GETTING INTO MONEY

A CAREER GUIDE

CHERI FEIN

BALLANTINE BOOKS

NEW YORK

FOR JULIAN
who's been with me from the start

Grateful acknowledgment is made to the following for permission to
reprint previously published material:

Dow Jones & Company, Inc.: excerpt from the article "Prosperity
and Peril in the Brave New Market" by M.R. Sesit, A. Monroe,
and P. Truell from *The Wall Street Journal.* Reprinted by permission of *The Wall Street Journal.* © Dow Jones & Company, Inc.,
1986. All Rights Reserved.
Institutional Investor Systems, Inc.: excerpts from charts which
appeared in "Ranking America's Biggest Brokers" from the April
1987 issue of *Institutional Investor.*

Library of Congress Catalog Card Number: 87-91555

ISBN: 0-345-34124-4

Cover design by Tony Russo
Photo: Image Bank
Book design by Beth Tondreau Design
Manufactured in the United States of America
First Edition: April 1988
10 9 8 7 6 5 4 3 2 1

PHOTO CREDITS
p. 54, *Katherine Updike:* Dave Schuessler Photography, Chicago; p. 116,
Barbara Thomas: RobertLam Color; p. 148, *Brenda Lee Landry:* Pach
Bros., New York. All other photographs courtesy of the subjects.

ACKNOWLEDGMENTS

This book would not have been possible without the help of the many people who so generously gave their time and shared their expertise. I would like to thank everyone who allowed me to interview them, both those whose names appear and those who are not directly quoted. Others allowed me to use their names so that doors would open. For that I am equally grateful. Many thanks to these friends and professionals who worked behind the scenes to make this book happen: Elizabeth Delude, Brad Gooch, Laurel Blossom, Tony Talalay, L. Kirk Payne, Sheila Small, Jim Feldman, Charlotte and Leonard Fein, Chris Cox, Bob Rubin, Angela Zizzi Daily, Ann Stark, Charles Brophy, Katherine McMillan, Michael Waber, Bob Freedman, Johanne Reid, Betsy Flagler, and Pat Eisemann.

I also want to thank my editor Joelle Delbourgo and assistants Elizabeth Cross, Philip Wiese, Stephanie Gaines, Kyle Engen, and Anne Isocowitz, and Julian's babysitter, Becky Fernandez. Their support was invaluable.

Special thanks to Tom Cassidy for his good spirit and extraordinary generosity.

Finally, my deepest gratitude to my husband George Gilbert, who stands by me through bull and bear markets.

CONTENTS

PART ONE
THE GAME

I always liked this business and I do not believe a man can succeed unless he loves his work. However, I am not prepared to give you any formula for success in Wall Street, as I believe every man must work out his own course. Of this I am certain—that no man can succeed who is not a worker and who does not value his integrity above all things.

—Arthur Salomon
a founder of Salomon Brothers
written in 1914

You only dream the thing that happened here this afternoon.
—Damon Runyon

CHAPTER 1

TAKING STOCK
OF THE
MONEY BUSINESS

"Your world should know no boundaries."
"Minds over money."
"Rock solid. Market wise."

D o these phrases refer to the men and women of Wall
Street? They could, you know. That they are instead slo-
gans for three of the largest firms—Merrill Lynch, Shearson/
Lehman Brothers, and Prudential-Bache—only underscores
the point: that it's ambitious, focused, savvy people who run
the financial machine without which other industries couldn't
operate. A startling thought? You bet it is. Imagine that your
job helps keep industry moving, thereby creating additional
jobs and strengthening the economy. That it flows with the
dollar and the United States' position in the world marketplace. That it's smack in the center of the universe. Because
that's where Wall Street is. It's not simply a geographical
point, a narrow street in lower Manhattan, but the heart that
keeps the world economy alive, the brain that keeps it thinking
and learning and growing.

You might as well know this right now—for the most part, the

3

men and women of Wall Street are not the money-grubbing
automatons so often portrayed in movies and bestselling fiction.
They are real flesh-and-blood people with tremendous drive and
energy, willing to give whatever it takes to plug into the powerful, high-stakes money game. They do what they do not only for
the considerable financial rewards, but because they love the
challenge. Again and again when talking with the high-powered
you hear them say, "I eat and sleep this job. I love it. If I didn't,
I couldn't possibly keep up the pace."

Investment bankers, brokers, traders, arbitrageurs, analysts,
venture capitalists—could you be one of them? Why not. Read
on and meet some of the players. Find out where the playing
fields are, what it takes to get a tryout, and how you can join
the team.

WHERE IS WALL STREET?

Physically, Wall Street is a narrow avenue, sun-blocked by office
towers, near the southern tip of Manhattan. Not surprisingly,
there once was an actual wall, but it's long gone. Today, Wall
Street is surrounded by other narrow streets with such names
as Broad, Nassau, William, and Pearl, and it functions not as a
city boundary but as the hot seat of the financial world.

Yet Wall Street, as it is generally spoken of, is far more than
office buildings on a few streets. Wall Street really is a euphe-
mism for the entire U.S. financial marketplace.

You can work on Wall Street and have your office in midtown
Manhattan along tony Park Avenue, as does First Boston. Or
you can sit on the southernmost tip of Manhattan, looking out
to the Statue of Liberty in New York Harbor, as do employees
of Salomon Brothers. Or you can watch the boats go by from
the newest addition to New York's financial skyline: the World
Financial Center, fourteen acres of offices, shops, and plazas
built on landfill along the Hudson River, where the likes of

Merrill Lynch, American Express, Daiwa Securities, Oppenheimer & Co., and Dow Jones & Co. have settled.

But Wall Street doesn't even restrict itself to Manhattan. Wall Street is Los Angeles, where Drexel Burnham Lambert has its junk bond financing department. It's Chicago, the pulse point of options, futures, and commodities trading. It's London and Tokyo and Paris and Mexico City.

Get the picture? Wall Street is not geography; it's an industry and a state of mind. It's the world. You can be a broker in St. Louis or an international banker in Singapore. You're still on Wall Street.

We can thank technology in large part for the expansion of Wall Street. Enormous amounts of information are amassed, digested, and exploited day by day, minute by minute, second by second as Telerate, Quotron, and Reuters screens flash in market centers around the world. It takes less time to find out what's happening halfway around the world than it does to walk from one room to another. Walter Wriston, former chairman of Citicorp, put it this way: "Mankind now has a completely integrated international financial and informational marketplace capable of moving money and ideas to any place on this earth in minutes." Wriston further noted that "the information standard has replaced the gold standard as the basis of world finance. The iron laws of the gold standard and later the gold exchange standard have been replaced by new laws which are just as inflexible. . . . It's also something that has made control impossible. Kings and princes can no longer hide what they're doing." Maybe. But kings and princes have never before been able to do so much.

WALL STREET AS IT'S NEVER BEEN BEFORE

There was a time, during Wall Street's White Shoe Era, when the financial game was a polite one, built on tradition. Investment banks stayed on one side, commercial banks stayed on the other. Brokerage houses played in their own area. In recent years, however, territorial definitions have blurred. While each institution used to have a specialized role, the lifting of numerous federal regulations has allowed the same services to become available from a variety of sources. Furthermore, new financial instruments seem to be invented every day. There's such an array of freshly boxed financial packages that it sets the mind spinning. Mortgage-backed securities, junk bonds, interest-rate swaps—the list goes on. Just as you think, "That's it. There's nothing new," another whiz kid comes up with something else to attract investors. Far more than merely a numbers cruncher, today's Wall Street professional is frequently wildy creative.

Partially as a result of all the crossover of business that deregulation has brought, and partially because it's become the way of the world, financial professionals have become specialists; the old jack-of-all-trades banker is a rare breed. With so much crossover, jobs are no longer defined so much by whom you work for as by what you do. An analyst covering the auto industry may be employed by an investment bank, or by a commercial bank, or directly by an automobile manufacturer. That person is still an analyst, and his or her area of expertise remains the same. Only the institution and what it will do with the information the analyst provides may be different.

Buy Side–Sell Side

There are two sides to the financial business: the buy side and the sell side. If you work for one of the Wall Street institutions—a brokerage house, a mutual fund company, a money management firm—you're on the sell side. If you work for an insurance company or some place that's not a financial institution, such as a corporation or a university, then you're on the buy side. When you think about it, the definitions make perfect sense. What's Wall Street's job? To sell its products and services. Who's buying? Insurance companies are investing their capital. Pension funds of corporations are investing that money. Schools and universities are investing what they have. Corporations have myriad needs—cash management, investment, mergers and acquisitions, underwriting, etc. All of these institutions have large amounts of capital, and they make up the bulk of Wall Street's business. They are the buyers, buying what Wall Street has to offer.

Now think back to that analyst job discussed above. If you're an analyst for a brokerage house, then you work on the sell side of the business. If you're employed as an analyst for a pension fund that invests, then you're on the buy side.

This book concentrates solely on the sell side of the business. But keep in mind that for many of the positions discussed you could just as well be working on the buy side. Knowing this multiplies your employment options.

Two Big Acts

There are two acts of Congress that you'll want to know about because they changed the nature of Wall Street. The first is the Glass–Steagall Act of 1933, and the second is the "May Day" deregulation of fixed commissions which took effect on May 1, 1975.

The Glass–Steagall Act established a wall between commercial banks and investment banks/brokerage houses; a wall which, despite crossover in many other areas of the business, remains. The Glass–Steagall Act came into existence during the Depression and mainly prohibits commercial banks from underwriting, a function that in this country remains with investment banks. This is not so outside of the U.S., however, which is one reason why American firms, like pioneers, have rushed to claim a piece of foreign turf.

A big change, and a welcome one for investors and consumers, was the 1975 deregulation of commissions, which dropped fixed commissions on transactions and instead allowed them to become negotiable. This set a whirl of competition in motion as firms began vying for clients. It also heralded the discount broker, a no-frills invention described in chapter 4.

BLACK MONDAY

For five years, the stock market soared, breaking record after record and rocketing the Dow by August 25, 1987 to an all-time high of 2,722.42. Jobs abounded; money was made, lots of money. It was the best of times. Yet when it comes to the stock market, what goes up must come down. This is a known truth, and by 1987 predictions were not "if" but "when." The answer came on October 19, when the Dow plunged a record 508 points, a 22.6 percent drop. Some called it a collapse or crash; others claimed it was a "necessary adjustment" to an inflated market. Everyone called it Black Monday.

Whatever it was, firms and individuals both were shaken by the sudden loss of substantial amounts of capital. "Retrenchment" became the operative word as some companies merged or even went out of business, and most trimmed their employee rosters. As William P. Hinckley, who was a trader at E.F. Hutton until it merged with Shearson/Lehman Brothers, told the *New York Times* on December 19, "You get paid a lot more than you're worth when things are good, and you're lucky to have a job when things are bad."

The question readers of this book will naturally ask is: In the wake of Black Monday, what are my chances of landing a good position? The answer? There isn't one answer. As of this writing, there certainly is much speculation about how the market decline will directly affect those who wish to work on Wall Street. At first glance things don't look particularly promising.

Reading about the consolidation of firms and about layoffs and hiring freezes can be disheartening. It is all the more important, then, to take in the following facts, which will lend balance to the situation:

- Despite year-end drops, the Dow Jones closed 1987 47 points higher than it started the year.
- On the first day of trading in 1988, the stock market gained 76 points. This was the fourth biggest rally ever.
- Competition between firms remains keen, and business is quite active. Where there is business, there are professionals taking care of that business. That means jobs.
- An unprecedented number of people making an unprecedented amount of money had gorged the financial world during the last bull market. Cutbacks are probably temporary, and hardly spell Ghost Town or Poor House for the industry.
- News item: Goldman Sachs reduced its 1987 year end bonus from 25 percent to 22 percent of base pay. Three whole percentage points on an already handsome base pay. Not exactly welfare money. And this cut affected support staff only.
- News item: In December 1987 Merrill Lynch announced a $200 million cut in overall salary costs, including a reduction in wage scales for its retail brokerage force. Sounds terrible, no? Well, the average compensation among the firm's 12,200 retail brokers is $110,000. Merrill's 6 percent cut in broker compensation represents an average salary loss of $6,600 per broker. That still leaves $103,400 a year. Not bad.

All of this is not to deny the seriousness of the October 19 drop. But in an unusually emotional market, perspective is important. Remember that the market does defy gravity: What goes down comes back up. How soon? Who knows. Perhaps by the time this book gets into your hands. Meanwhile, bull or bear market, there *always* are opportunities on Wall Street for those who belong there.

THE NEW WALL STREET

For many years Wall Street had the reputation of being a clubby, gentlemen's business. It ran on school-tie friendships and established relationships. It ran on who knew whom and who came from where. Firms, many of them family owned, were sharply divided by background, so that a firm that pulled clients from one ethnic group would not likely pull from another. Everyone had his territory, and mostly that was just fine. There was room on the Street for more than one private club. As for the atmosphere of the Street itself, it was quite different from today's hubbub. Ken Auletta described it this way in his excellent book, *Greed and Glory on Wall Street:*

> Two decades ago, markets were stable, interest costs and inflation low, the overhead of firms was small, fees were steady, competition gentlemanly, and government regulations paced approval for underwritings; companies were rarely menaced by hostile takeovers, there was "no such thing as positioning a private placement," no risky trading of bonds in secondary markets, and certificates of deposit were just beginning.

But all that has changed. Today the doors have swung wide open, and the rules of the game have been updated. Although it never hurts to have contacts, it's no longer so much who you know but what you can do. It's not where you come from but where you're going. You have to prove yourself, show your talent, and only then can you join the team. The catchwords you hear—bottom line, aggressive, dynamic, creative, competitive—tell part of the story. Today's players are tougher and smarter than ever before. They are young go-getters with a fire inside. They work hard, very hard, and afterwards they mostly play hard. If love makes the world go round, one could argue quite persuasively that it's love of money that keeps the investment community spinning. Not just money as in a fat paycheck, though there's certainly that, but love of spending hard-working hours flexing financial muscles and having a direct affect on the world's big plays.

When you picture a banker, what do you see? A guy in a dark gray, boxy suit, white shirt, polished black shoes. Maybe he's wearing a red tie if he's a powerhouse type, but otherwise something pretty dull. The woman you picture also wears a suit and one of those silky blouses with some kind of bow at the neck. Her pumps are sensible, her stockings neutral. She wears pearls, and her hair is plain. Maybe she wears a dress instead of a suit, but it's hardly an adventurous style. It's true that with rare exceptions these "uniforms" are the rule. But don't be deceived by the book's cover. There's nothing stodgy about the manner in which young Wall Streeters conduct their professional lives. On the job they are sharp as tacks and they don't give up. They do whatever needs to be done, and they do it long after sleepy souls have turned in for the night. No one who gives less than his or her best—and then some—has a chance of making it in today's competitive marketplace.

THE FIRMS

Sure there are the Big Guys, and we'll name them here. But great as these giants are, big doesn't translate necessarily to best. It would be impossible to list all the companies that serve the financial community; there simply are too many located across the country. Just keep in mind, after you've taken a look at the Old and Powerful, that there are also many exciting and profitable specialty boutiques. Maybe a supermarket like Merrill Lynch is just the place for you. But maybe a less widely known powerhouse like Baltimore-based Alex Brown or Minneapolis's Piper Jaffray or Robinson Humphrey in Atlanta or St. Louis's A. G. Edwards is better suited to your talents.

Some of the top money-makers in this country lead companies you've probably never heard of. Take George Soros, for example, president of Soros Fund Management. According to *Financial World* (July 22, 1986), Soros made $93.5 million in profits, fees, and bonuses from his Netherlands Antilles-based Quantum Fund in the previous year. And have you heard of Junction Partners? This low-key, New York-based arbitrage company's managing partner, Jeffrey Tarr, took home somewhere between $30 million and $40 million in 1985. Yet Tarr claimed that in the first quarter of 1986 he did even better than in all of 1985! Then there's Jamie Securities, a risk arbitrage company, whose general partner John Mulheren (a thirty-nine-year-old Bruce Springsteen fan) reportedly earns double-digit millions each year.

But getting back to the best-known big guns, the top six investment houses that garner most of the deals are known as the "bulge bracket." Together they underwrite about 60 percent of the new securities floated by investment grade companies. They are:

Merrill Lynch, Pierce, Fenner & Smith. Founded 1914. Absolutely huge; a financial supermarket. Famous for its excellent training programs.

Shearson/Lehman Brothers. Founded 1960. Became a giant in a short amount of time, largely by gobbling up some twenty other investment firms, including the venerable Lehman Brothers. Most recently merged with E. F. Hutton.

Salomon Brothers. Founded 1910. Famous for its huge trading floor and tough, aggressive reputation.

Goldman, Sachs & Co. Founded 1869. Known as one of the best run firms on Wall Street. A strong emphasis on teamwork, though shaken up a bit by the recent insider trading scandal.

Morgan Stanley & Co. Founded 1935. Once a blue-chip, button-down, very clubby firm, the aura remains in this new era, even as not-so-polite big deals are affected.

The First Boston Corp. Founded 1934. Where many of the
new flock of Wall Streeters apply. America's first publicly
owned investment bank, and still one of the best.

Those may be the all-time biggies, but the list continues with
other firms, also of considerable size and influence. They are,
in no particular order:

Dean Witter Reynolds
PaineWebber
Prudential-Bache
Bear, Stearns
Donaldson, Lufkin & Jenrette
Drexel Burnham Lambert
Kidder, Peabody
Thomson McKinnon
Smith Barney, Harris Upham
Neuberger & Berman
Oppenheimer & Co.
L. F. Rothschild, Unterberg, Towbin
Allen & Co.
Brown Brothers Harriman
Dillon, Read & Co.
Lazard Frères
Wertheim & Co.

And then there are the commercial banks—Citicorp, Bankers
Trust, Wells Fargo, BankAmerica, Security Pacific, First Inter-
state, Chase Manhattan Bank, Chemical Bank, Manufacturers
Hanover Trust, not to mention the many regional and smaller
banks and expanding thrift institutions. There are literally thousands of companies that specialize in such services as mutual
funds or tax-advantaged investments or portfolio management.
The list of companies that serve individuals and smaller businesses, as well as those that provide services to the big institutions themselves, goes on and on.

IS NEW YORK THE ONLY PLACE?

Yes . . . and no. Certainly New York is this country's financial capital and still the world heavyweight champion (in competition with Tokyo and London). And yes, it's the place you want to be for the top research analyst programs and summer jobs and training programs. In terms of numbers alone, New York is the land of opportunity, offering more employment options than any other U.S. city. By the middle of 1987, according to the Federal Bureau of Labor Statistics, the financial industry had become the fifth-largest in the city, employing more than 150,000 people in every area, from stockbrokers and floor traders to computer operators and clerical workers. Even with post–Black Monday layoffs, New York holds the lead.

On the other hand, it's important to know that the rest of the country is far from a wasteland. All of the major firms—Shearson, Merrill Lynch, Dean Witter, to name a few—and many of the smaller ones have offices throughout the country. Just take a peek at chapter 4 for an indication of the huge number of stockbrokers working in the big firms' many branch offices. Add to that the investment bankers, money managers, analysts, venture capitalists, traders, operations staffs, and the like, and you'll quickly see that plenty of people have made the decision not to congregate on the Isle of Manhattan.

And there's often absolutely no need to. Individuals and companies everywhere, not just in New York, have financial needs. A stockbroker's work relies on finding clients with money to invest. If you're a money manager or trust officer, you simply have to be where people have money that needs managing. Anyplace with a large bank will have trust and money management work. Look particularly to Boston, Philadelphia, Hartford, and San Francisco for key positions in money management, since the biggest insurance companies are located in these cities. Boston is also the original home of mutual funds, and is still quite strong in that area. Fidelity, Keystone, Massachusetts Financial Services, and Putnam are all located there.

Top securities analyst Perrin Long points out that despite all the publicity about New York investment banks, there are many securities firms located all over the country. He notes that at the end of March 1987, there were 388 New York Stock Exchange member firms doing business with the public; of these the majority were located west of the Hudson. These firms, Long says, tend to have higher profit margins before taxes than the New York firms, and, not surprisingly, lower overhead.

Other types of jobs require a particular geographic location. If you're a commodities trader, for instance, Chicago may be the place for you, since it's home to the major options, futures, and commodities exchanges. Philadelphia and San Francisco also have active options, futures, and commodities exchanges. Toronto is becoming an important trading center, too. If you're a venture capitalist, you may want to look in or around Boston or near California's Silicon Valley, where much of the new technology is based.

There always are individuals who just aren't ready or willing to settle in New York. That doesn't stop them from developing their businesses, and doing a great job of it. San Francisco's Montgomery Securities, founded in 1971 and one of the top U.S. investment firms, reportedly conducts more business than any other stock firm outside Wall Street. Also in San Francisco is Hellman & Friedman, a "boutique" investment bank that often spends months getting to know the concerns and corporate culture of clients such as Levi Straus. Other important regional investment firms that have given New York a "nay" include Robinson Humphrey, of Atlanta; Stephens Inc., of Little Rock, Arkansas; A. G. Edwards & Sons, of St. Louis; and Blair & Co. and Van Kampen Merritt, both of Chicago.

Money managers Richard McKenzie and Stephen Walker of McKenzie–Walker Investment Management work from Larkspur, California, where each earned, according to *Financial World* (July 22, 1986), a reported $20 million plus in 1985. Now that's success. And although venture capitalist David Dunn grew up in Brooklyn, he now lives and works in Fort Worth, Texas.

As Dunn told the Harvard Business School *Bulletin,* and it holds true for many go-getters who have chosen not to do battle in Manhattan, "It doesn't much matter where you locate, as long as you're near a good airport."

The fact is that with the advancements of technology anyone, anywhere can keep up with the action. For an indication of how far telecommunications has taken us, look at Hambrecht & Quist. Headquartered in San Francisco, but with offices in New York, Boston, and Los Angeles, Hambrecht & Quist has set up video conference rooms in its offices. Each room has the typical conference table and chairs, plus large video monitors that connect people from the various offices. It's an extraordinary system. Gordon S. Macklin, chairman of Hambrecht & Quist, explains that the video conference room is regularly used for meetings of the managing directors, who work out of the four offices. "When a meeting is called," Macklin says, "we don't fly those people to San Francisco. We all go to our conference rooms, sit down, turn on our machines, and chat just as if we were all in the same room."

The video conference room is also used to simplify the process of determining which securities the company will underwrite. "We underwrite a lot," notes Macklin. "And to underwrite a lot you first have to look at a heck of a lot. You just can't run and gather in one place all the time. But we don't need to. We set an agreed upon time, go to our conference rooms, sit down. Whoever is introducing the company at hand introduces the subject matter. It may be a corporate finance person in San Francisco, supported by a specialized research person in New York. The corporate finance person will speak, then the research person 3,000 miles away will speak. We're all looking right at them."

Gordon Macklin is right on target when he says that "the days of needing to be in one central place are rapidly passing. Frankly, the secret of a good business is being close to your customers."

For many people, the secret to being content in their business is having a comfortable lifestyle, and for them, that means "not New York." As one Philadelphia trader puts it, "I'm under constant pressure and tension. I'm physically and emotionally drained by the end of the day and certainly by the end of the week. It means a lot to me to live in a beautiful home in a wonderful area only fifteen minutes from work. I can get home to my wife and children, and I don't spend half my life on the road."

Investment banker Katherine Updike, who works out of Chicago for Chase Manhattan, feels that that city has quite a bit to offer. "One of the real attractions of Chicago is that it is a major market. You certainly have the opportunity to be employed with some of the best and brightest in the industry, in trading, corporate finance, you name it. Plus you have a very palatable lifestyle, close to the city, close to where you work. That's an attraction that certainly doesn't escape a lot of people."

Yet other people leave or bypass New York as part of their career strategy. William C. Nelson, executive director of First Republic Bank Corporation, grew up in Ohio and graduated from Yale with a degree in history. After interviewing in New York and elsewhere, he accepted a position at the Mellon Bank in Pittsburgh, not, as he says, "because it was a more limited organization, but because at that time, in 1960, it looked to me like one could make his mark sooner there." Even today, Nelson figures, if you get your grounding at a place like Morgan or Citibank in New York, and then move on to a city like Pittsburgh or Cleveland or Charlotte or Dallas, "you'll probably be a real star, because you can leverage what you've learned on Wall Street and move more quickly in a regional bank."

Nelson points out that consumer and middle market banking—making loans, financing autos, dealing with credit card and deposit activities, handling private banking services for wealthy individuals and small businesses—is done all over the U.S. So are other banking areas, such as trusts, operations, general lending to multinational companies, and overseas work. "It's a question," he says, "of where you want to live and where you see the opportunities."

Katherine Updike agrees that the opportunities can most definitely be found outside New York. From her vantage point in Chicago, she sees how both regionally based investment banks and commercial banks are grabbing onto the business in the Midwest, and, in reaction to that, how the New York firms are moving their people into the region. "If you take [the Chicago investment firm] William Blair, for instance, which has been incredibly good at identifying emerging companies, companies that are going public in the region, you'll see that they are able to hold onto those companies a lot longer than they used to. And as the commercial banks that are already residents here begin to do debt offerings and the international business and the rate arbitrage business, all of a sudden your Salomons and Merrills and Morgan Stanleys are saying, 'My gosh, we're losing that traditional field. As those companies begin to stretch a William Blair's capabilities, they're not necessarily coming to us in New York. We've got to get more active in targeting and identifying [their needs] earlier.' So I think that is forcing the business to be delivered a lot differently than it used to be, and I suspect it's one of the reasons you're seeing the opportunities outside Wall Street. You're now seeing traditional New York investment banks put in regional staff. There are very active, very successful people in Chicago, Minneapolis, St. Louis, Indianapolis, and Milwaukee, just to talk about this region."

In the chapters ahead, you'll meet Gordon Macklin and Bill Nelson and Katie Updike again. You'll also meet other people, like Cincinnati stockbroker Scott Randall; Drexel Burnham Lambert's legendary Mike Milken, who works out of Los Angeles; and Chicago's super commodities trader Richard Dennis. They, among others, are proof positive that success knows no geographic boundaries.

A WOMAN'S PLACE

In its clubby days, Wall Street was a male bastion, but as you read earlier in this chapter, that has changed considerably. Take Muriel Siebert, for example. She was the first woman to buy a seat on the New York Stock Exchange. That was in 1967. Shortly thereafter, Siebert became the first woman to trade on the floor of the exchange. Today, about one-third of Wall Street's younger professionals are women.

There's no question that women have poked holes in Wall Street's walls. Siebert now has her own discount brokerage firm. You will meet other terrific, successful women in the chapters that follow. They raise the question: Are opportunities for women equal to those for men?

The answer is that they are indeed in some areas . . . and they aren't in others. The bad news first. Starting at the top. Can you guess how many of the 600 managing directors or partners in the top-drawer investment firms in 1986 were women? Seven. Less than one percent. And as for incomes, of the 100 people listed in *Financial World's* "The Highest Paid People on Wall Street" (July 22, 1986), none was a woman. In *Working Woman's* July 1986 article on the ten worst careers for women, number six was investment banking. Here's what that magazine had to say on the subject: "Grueling hours and intense pressure make investment banking an unfriendly place for both genders. But the prevailing attitude that boardroom dramas and highrolling deals are no place for a lady causes special problems for women."

This doesn't mean that there are no women investment bankers. There are, in fact, quite a few, and they make a lot of money, several hundred thousand dollars a year on average. But you can be sure that on the employment–salary seesaw, the men are overly weighted, while the women are hanging lightly in the air. According to a study conducted by the Columbia University School of Business, male and female MBAs with matching qualifications start out on Wall Street and elsewhere at the same salary. But within ten years, the women have fallen behind by 20 percent, regardless of the company they work for or their jobs. As for a woman's chances for advancement to truly high places, the statistics cited above speak for themselves.

In the other hot seat, hotshot areas—mergers and acquisitions, arbitrage, leveraged buyouts—how often do women's names come up? Think of the most famous corporate raiders— T. Boone Pickens, Saul Steinberg, Carl Icahn, Asher Edelman, Carl Lindner—no women there. For that matter, think of those who have been caught in the famous insider trading scandal that first sent shock waves through the financial community in 1986. The first to be nabbed was Dennis Levine; the most famous was Ivan Boesky. No women there, thank heavens. It wouldn't help the image-building one bit.

On the upside, the changed and changing nature of Wall Street bodes well for the future of women. With lessening emphasis on the Old Boy network and greater emphasis on the bottom line, firms increasingly are seeking the brightest talent they can find, and they don't care if you're male, female, goat, or giraffe, as long as you can do the job. Says one recruiter for a prestigious firm, "We're in this to make money. Period. I'll take on whoever can help us meet that objective."

Women also are making their way through business school at a furious pace. Just a little more than a decade ago, scarcely one newly minted MBA in eight was a woman. Today it's one in three. That means there are more highly trained, talented women competing with men for positions. They have started to be and will continue to be recognized.

If the world of investment banking is still fairly grim for women, commercial banking looks better. In the same issue of *Working Woman* that listed investment banking as one of the ten worst professions for women, another piece on the twenty-five hottest careers named commercial banking. It's encouraging to note that almost half of all bank officers and managers are women. At Wells Fargo Bank, women make up 75 percent of the work force and 65 percent of management. Working as a financial planner or as a financial public-relations executive were also named as hot careers.

As you read on you'll read about women who are brokers, analysts, venture capitalists, traders, international bankers. Some are in extremely powerful positions. All are doing very, very well. Most important, each one says she loves her profession, and of all the rewards, that—for both men and women—is the greatest.

CHAPTER 2

WOOING THE
TALENTED

Sure the competition for terrific jobs is stiff, but the financial industry is always on the lookout for bright achievers. And in the grand style it's become accustomed to, Wall Street woos the talented in a big way. Both on campus and on their own turf, recruiters for top firms campaign with words and wine, inviting those they are interested in to expensively prepared events. Lavish dinners at fine restaurants and trendy clubs, moonlit cruise-cocktail parties up the Hudson River, limos to whisk you back to your hotel—these are common in Wall Street's quest for this year's best. During times when the market is shaky and some firms are watching their pocketbooks more closely, the wooing may be toned down. In the worst of times, hiring may even appear to grind to a halt. Don't be deceived. Without players, there is no game.

The game is played from both sides: investment and commercial banks try to impress young people so that they'll want to come work for them; meanwhile, would-be Wall Streeters, eager for job offers, work hard to impress their seniors. As you can imagine, everyone is on his best behavior.

Who is being recruited and where? Both undergrads and business school students, on campus and on the job. On campus, recruiters often hold open sessions, which anyone can attend, and individual interviews and by-invitation-only events for those deemed the most promising. This "most promising" group may then be brought to New York for more interviewing and wining and dining. Summer interns—MBA students who are working on Wall Street during their summer vacations—are also actively wooed by competing firms, for when they graduate they'll be looking for permanent positions, and not necessarily at the firms where they spent their summer.

In recent years events sponsored by the firms and designed to impress young talent have become increasingly grand. It's not unheard of for a bank to spend $10,000 on a single party. And the parties abound. During the summer, you can go to one almost every night. Clearly it's a great way to get a free meal, but more important, it's a great way to get a feel for each firm's "corporate culture," or its ambiance. And if you like what you see, it's the place to position yourself for an interview by chatting up the right people.

Despite their fun facade, you can be sure that financial institutions are not spending this kind of money simply to have a good time. There's no question that these parties are serious business. First of all, there are a lot of young people who want to come to Wall Street, and one task of the firms is to figure out who they want from this flock. To get some idea of how popular Wall Street is these days, take a look at these statistics: in 1986, fully half of Yale's undergraduate class wanted to work in the financial industry; nearly one-third of Harvard Business School's 1987 graduates found jobs with investment banking firms up from one-quarter the previous year; and finally, investment banks attracted three times as many Harvard MBAs in 1986 as did industrial companies. This last figure is a complete reversal of the way things stood in 1979. As if this news isn't daunting enough, you might want to know that there are more MBAs than ever before. In 1986 a record 71,000 MBAs burst forth from campuses around the country. That's nearly a 30 percent jump from 1980. So the coffers have been filling with golden boys and girls on their way to the "Big Time."

Now trends can and do change, and as a result of Black Monday the rush to Wall Street might slow. For those committed to a career in the financial world, any trend shifts that might occur will have little effect—except perhaps to make it a bit easier to land a position.

The average age of Wall Street professionals has been getting younger. "Easily 50 percent of Wall Street is thirty-five or under," speculated Kevin Sullivan, president of Kevin Sullivan Associates, a New York executive recruiting firm that specializes in financial services, to the *New York Times* on August 9, 1987. The newspaper reported in that same article that Fidelity Investments in Boston has entrusted its $83.5 billion in assets to sixty portfolio managers whose average age is thirty-six. But several of the portfolio managers on the Fidelity Select mutual funds, the high-profile sector funds that invest in narrow industry groups, are as young as twenty-six.

As for hiring trends, most firms are taking on more MBAs. In 1986, Salomon Brothers led the pack by hiring forty-six. Morgan Stanley was second with thirty-six, with Merrill Lynch's thirty-five bringing up a close third. Goldman Sachs brought in thirty-two, and First Boston thirty. Still, that's a mere 179 out of the thousands who applied, so back to the competition issue—it's tough out there on Wall Street.

Taking a look at geographical distribution, a spokesman for Drexel Burnham Lambert reports that twenty-six MBAs were hired by that company in 1986. Of that group, fifteen started in New York, eight in Los Angeles, two in Boston, and one in San Francisco. The Boston and San Francisco positions were firsts, because Drexel is trying to build up regional offices there. About why New York remains the place where most new people start, the spokesman says that since on-the-job training is so crucial, most investment banking firms feel that it's best to start where the majority of the big deals take place. Another recruiter put it this way: "Most firms still require that you start out in New York. It's the typical career path. New York hires more people than anywhere else in the country, so if you're really serious about getting into this business, plan on spending at least a few years in the Big Apple." Of course, there's no saying that you have to work for one of the biggest firms. Chapter 1 mentions some of the smaller companies, where the rewards may be at least as great.

Speaking of rewards, there's no question that, financially speaking, they are substantial. Undergraduates starting out in commercial banking or perhaps in research for an investment bank are likely to start at $18,000. That's not bad, and it's the low end of the business. Young men and women in investment banking research analyst programs start at around $30,000. Investment bankers with MBAs can expect to start at $60,000 to $80,000 and see $100,000 by their second year. And practically everyone on Wall Street makes six figures very early in their careers. It's heady stuff.

Just what are you expected to give back for such a generous salary, you might well ask? For a sense of that, let's go directly to the beautifully produced booklets that three players—Citicorp, Merrill Lynch, and Drexel Burnham Lambert—provide for people who are interested in their firms. There you'll find direct quotes from the people who count: your future bosses.

> In this business, we need people who are leaders, not followers—people who have a high degree of enthusiasm and motivation. Of course, they have to be bright, but they also have to be creative in their approach to problem solving. Open-mindedness is also important, as are good interpersonal skills and teamwork. Most of all, we need people who can get excited about searching out opportunities, assuming responsibility, confronting challenges and succeeding with a high standard of excellence.
>
> —Alan S. MacDonald
> Head of the North American Investment Bank
> Citicorp

> We look for people who are articulate, aggressive, can take calculated risks, have had some prior Street experience, and know about Merrill Lynch. We also look for an added some-

thing that shows they're ambitious—like running their own summer business or financing some of their education.

—Samuel E. Hunter
Senior Vice President, Securities Trading
Merrill Lynch

Government securities isn't the kind of business you can walk away from at five o'clock. It's a 24-hour job and it's my hobby. ... You have to be very innovative to attract customers in this market. The 20 or so professionals who work with me combine innovation, experience and the commitment it takes to help clients make sound decisions about their portfolios. . . . I'm proud of the way our people work toward common goals. This helps to give us the edge over everyone else out there.

—Michael (Jack) Kugler
Vice Chairman, Chief Executive Officer
Drexel Burnham Lambert Government Securities Inc.

ROBERT LINTON
CHAIRMAN, DREXEL BURNHAM LAMBERT

Robert Linton, chairman of the daring and aggressive Drexel Burnham Lambert, has been known to say that it is not a single product or idea that makes his Wall Street firm great, but the people who work for him. Once he's got good people, Linton believes in turning them loose and intervening only when necessary. Obviously, this philosophy works; Drexel has experienced explosive growth in the last half dozen years, most notably in its development of the controversial but highly profitable junk bond market, but also in other areas. (Junk bonds are below-investment grade bonds that yield above-average returns for investors; they are a way for smaller, high-growth companies to raise capital.)

The corporate culture at Drexel is different from that at most other Wall Street firms. Purposely understated, there are no limos, no designer-decorated offices. There's relatively little jealousy among colleagues. It's a place where loners and original thinkers reportedly can not only find a spot but develop to their full potential. The bottom line is that Drexel is no snob club. It's out to make money, and it does.

A lifetime employee of the firm, Linton is the one who sets this mood, and he maintains it—despite the fact that he's passed on the job of chief executive officer to Frederick Joseph, his likely successor. So successful has Linton been that in 1985 he was named Institutional Investor's Banker of the Year. This was the first time Institutional Investor selected an investment banker instead of a commercial banker for that award. Business Week has described Linton as "gruff and supremely self-confident." These qualities no doubt surface when necessary, but just as often, Linton reveals a warm and relaxed side. Far from showy, Linton's office is outfitted more for comfort than style and is free from the trappings usually associated with the position of chairman. There's no original art on his walls; instead you see posters of Drexel's print ads. His sofa is well worn, and his desk is cluttered.

Linton started out in 1946, when he decided to skip college and head directly for a modest job at the small firm of Burnham & Co. He didn't have to go that route. His family was well-to-do, and *he attended prep school—the exclusive Phillips Exeter Academy. Furthermore, Linton's father worked on Wall Street, so it would have been relatively easy for Linton to plug into a position with him. Instead, he made his own way over the years, working as a runner, a floor trader, a back-office clerk, a stockbroker, a research analyst, and an investment banker, thereby learning the business literally from the bottom up. He also set up the corporate finance and commodities departments for his firm. Finally, in 1977 he was named president and chief executive officer. In 1982 he became chairman of the board.*

Clearly proud of his long term at Drexel and of the firm's growth, Linton keeps his collection of Drexel annual reports on a nearby shelf, starting with the first one issued in 1952. Compared with today's glossy affairs, it's a simple presentation—a mere five-page booklet, whose first paragraph, entitled "Progress," reads: "Since April 1, 1935, when Burnham & Co. first opened its doors, there's been a steady growth in the firm's business. The original 3 employees and 2 partners now number 71 employees and 10 partners. The net worth has increased from approximately $100,000 to the current $1,725,572.61."

As of this writing, Drexel Burnham Lambert's capital exceeds $2 billion.

Q: I understand that you've been at Drexel Burnham Lambert for over forty years.

A: Yes. I started at Burnham & Co. on January 2, 1946, when I got out of the service.

Q: By today's standards you've had an unusual history, in that you didn't go to college and came straight into this industry, starting as a runner. What was it like then?

A: I remember quite clearly that I started for $25 a week, which was considered quite generous at that time. My father was a specialist on the floor of the stock exchange, and the original idea was that I would learn the business upstairs and then go down on the floor. So I went into what de facto was an on-the-job training program. Within the first year, I went down on the floor as the assistant floor clerk for Burnham & Co. and realized after a few months that I had no interest in spending my life on the floor of the stock exchange. So I've just stayed with Burnham & Co. ever since. I spent two or three years in all the operations departments, which were one- or two-man departments, went in as the assistant to the partner who was the investment advisor and worked with him for five years. It was just him and myself and a secretary. I had a long number of years really learning the money management and investment advisory end of a very small firm, all the time registered and doing some business myself. Then I became assistant to Mark Edersheim [one of the partners] when he joined the firm. Somebody had to work with him; he was Dutch and didn't know our ways. Then I started what is now the corporate finance department during the late '50s. Until that time the deals had been done ad hoc. If a partner had a deal to do, he would pretty much work on it himself. So I went out and hired a lawyer and my secretary, Ruth, who has been with me for thirty-one years, and then spent many happy years developing and running a small, what we then called, industrial department. I became a partner in the firm in 1956.

Q: You became a partner after ten years. That's a pretty quick rise.

A: Well, it was a small firm. Business at that time was much simpler and slower. Then I went on as a general partner in charge of several operating departments, plus corporate finance, until the big change in the 1970s when I started the commodities department. I studied that and decided we should be in it. I had been on the executive committee by then for a number of years. I went on some time in the '60s, I guess, and was one of the senior partners of a small partnership. I became CEO [chief executive officer] in August 1977, which is about when our real growth started. In 1977 we did about $140 million of business. This year [1986] we'll do over $4 billion in business. I decided a while back that I would use my sixtieth birthday, which was May 1985, to step down as CEO.

Q: Why?

A: Because I think that most CEOs overstay their welcome in several senses. First of all, I believe in an orderly transition in companies, that you shouldn't wait until you die or are kicked out or are too old and people are trying to push you out. That you should do it while you're still active and involved, and can work with the new CEO and have a transitional period, so that you're there to quash any jealousies or positioning or problems that might arise. Second, I'm a great believer that your energy level and your outlook change considerably as you get older. The person I chose [Frederick Joseph] was forty-eight; I was sixty. I think that you should have younger people running businesses, in general. I have stayed as chairman of the board, chairman of the executive committee, chairman of the committee that meets every morning that really runs the business every day, and all my other titles I will gradually step down from. My successor, Fred Joseph, is doing a fabulous job, so I'm now on the downslope of this long career. By choice. And I will stay chairman of the board for as long as it suits me and it suits my associates.

Q: So you're not necessarily planning on leaving at sixty-five.

A: No. We have no mandatory retirement, and actually it would be a shame. In this business, all other things being equal, you get more and more valuable. Your contacts are constantly broadening; you get better and better known; you travel more, meet people in your industry. Outside political people you've known for a lot of years become important.

The people you knew in various regulatory agencies become head of them, and so on. So I don't believe at all in going out to pasture, putting aside any psychological aspects of that. As far as the benefits of the business are concerned, I think it's a good idea to stay as long as you're sure you want to do it, at least as chairman of the board.

Q: Was it always your ambition to be CEO?

A: No, it was nothing planned. I never thought about a career path or anything like that. It just happened. In a business like ours, circumstances have more do with management and management succession than anything else. It's not analogous to normal corporate life, where you work your way up the ladder. It just doesn't happen that way.

Q: What about these days? Things have changed radically, and the young people coming in today seem to be on a very specific track.

A: The big change is that now we have a world of specialists. Nobody would come into the business as I did and have a five-year apprenticeship. The people who go into investment banking or research or specialized trading devote themselves entirely to one aspect of the business. Therefore, it becomes harder to find people who are broadly trained. We try, wherever possible, to move management people around, but that's not easy. If you have somebody running a department and doing it well, it's a big sacrifice to take him out. of that department. But we do it from time to time. It's been part of our ability to develop successor managers.

Q: What is your opinion of the young people coming in today?

A: If you're talking about investment banking, they work very hard and seem to adapt very quickly to a lifestyle where there's little personal pleasure in the early years. They devote themselves almost entirely to their business. They're

very clever, very bright, and very narrow in their outlook. I
think the opportunity to broaden themselves intellectually in
terms of reading and art and theater and music and to broaden
their contacts outside the business world, to get involved in
politics and industry matters and so on, is sadly lacking by dint
of the fact that in those years they're devoting their entire
efforts to a very narrow direction. I think the same is true,
to a lesser extent, of people who come into research. And
then at the other end of the spectrum, you have the trading
people, who may come off the streets of New York from some
tough neighborhood and may or may not have finished high
school. You just never know who is going to turn out to have
what it takes to be a good trader. They're a completely different breed of people, and their lifestyles are very different.

Q: Some people are troubled by the young investment
banker's life, and yet the industry has created it.

A: I have four children, and I certainly would not encourage
them to get into a lifestyle where they were working seventy
or eighty hours a week and didn't have time to date and take
vacations and enjoy themselves. I believe in hard work. I've
worked very hard pretty much all my life, since I was seventeen, so it isn't a question of ethics. I just think it's a shame
that the morés have gone as far as they have. Now as an
employer and an owner of a firm that is a major investment
bank, it's wonderful. We get terrific value out of these young
people. But only time will tell what they'll be worth when
they're forty and fifty years old. I don't know the answer to
that. But they really have no choice at this point. It's a very
competitive world, and the jobs are going to be taken by those
who are willing to put out the most energy and devote themselves to it.

Q: What personal qualities have contributed to your success?

A: Well, it's hard to be modest and answer that. Handsome,

bright, hardworking . . . no, well, I would say first of all that
I've always taken my work very seriously and always been
very conscientious. If there was work to do on weekends or
at night or trips to be taken, it never even occurred to me
. . . we were brought up to do what we were told to do, or
asked to do. So I never questioned any task that was put in
front of me.

Second, I would say that I have a tremendous curiosity.
I've always been an avid reader of all different kinds of things,
not just business related. I'm an enthusiastic traveler, very
interested in the cultures and histories of other parts of the
world, as well as our own. Also, I'm an avid sportsman. I've
skied enthusiastically for over thirty years, and a lot of business and political friends have come out of that. I'm a great
believer in extracurricular activities. They all tie in closely
with a business that is basically a financial services business.
So I think a broad outlook has been helpful.

I've never cared about money per se. I think it comes more
easily to people who feel that way than to people who seek
it. If you do a good job, [the money] develops secondarily.
This firm, which is the most profitable firm in our industry and
may be the most profitable privately owned firm in the United
States, doesn't own a car or have a chauffeur, much less an
airplane. That's our style. We don't pay for people's country
clubs, and we don't have fancy offices. This is a place of
business. We enjoy it. We're competitive. We enjoy each
other. Everybody here who has something to offer makes a
lot of money. And if they want to go out and buy themselves
a Rolls Royce, that's up to them. But the style of the firm is
a pure meritocracy. It's very serious. If you don't pull your
oar around here, you don't make it. We don't have people who
are living off the fat of others. That's the way it's been for this
whole forty plus years, and hopefully, how it will continue to
be. It was Mr. Burnham's style, and it's my style. We're the
only two to have run this firm, and I think that's become part
of the culture of the firm.

Q: What kind of room is there for women?

A: It's increasing. We have our share of young women, and it becomes a unisex kind of approach. But there's much more of a weeding out process as the years go on. The percentage, as I observe it, of women who are willing to give up pretty much of their personal and private lives over a period of time is not as great as it is among the men. I think the opportunities at this point are equal, if they come out of school with equal credentials and recommendations. But I think the percentage that seem to be choosing to follow through after a period of, say, five years is quite a bit less. Perhaps the women are more sensible than the men in the way they perceive what life is about.

Q: What would you stress to young people coming into this business?

A: I would tell them to try very hard to broaden their horizons and not let themselves get swept entirely into the one narrow field that they're in. Not to give up reading the sports section and the theater section and some good literature and enjoying the arts in New York. I'd try to leave work one night a week to go to Lincoln Center. I mean, if they're going to make it beyond the first phase, I think they're going to need a lot of resources to fall back on beyond just becoming an investment banker. I think if you make an effort to plan your time, you can accomplish a great deal, and I wouldn't give up a fairly normal personal life either. I think you really have to think through on a long-term basis what life is all about beyond the narrow devotion for several years to something that isn't going to stand you well as an exclusive interest for the rest of your life.

Q: Is this realistic, though, given the hours people need to work?

A: I would think that somebody who is bright and organized could handle that. In my opinion, there's a huge amount of wasted time from disorganization, from lack of thought and lack of planning. I see it right and left. So I think a person can increase his efficiency tremendously if he really thinks through what he's going to give himself, rather than just being an automaton and letting it happen.

THE ETHICS ISSUE

"Quis custodiet ipsos custodes?" the Roman satirist Juvenal posed. Who will watch the watchers?

The pressure to succeed is phenomenal, and often the measure of success is how much money you're making compared to your peers. The dollar figures constantly being bandied about for big time deals are so staggering that after a while they seem like play money. The advance information you're privy to is mind-boggling. Little wonder that terrific men and women who seemingly have the world on a string sometimes lose their way. It's a real danger of running on the fast track, and one to keep firmly in mind.

The most shocking Wall Street scandal in many years, and possibly ever, hit in May 1986 when the Securities and Exchange Commission charged Dennis B. Levine of Drexel Burnham Lambert with making $12.6 million over the previous six years by trading illegally on inside information. (In August 1987 the Securities and Exchange Commission spelled out a definition of insider trading. That definition, in part, states that "it shall be unlawful for any person, directly or indirectly, to purchase, sell, or cause the purchase or sale of, any security while in possession of material nonpublic information concerning the issuer or its securities, if such person knows or recklessly disregards that such information has been obtained wrongfully or that such purchase or sale would constitute a wrongful use of such information.") It should be noted that the $12.6 million Levine made was above and beyond his considerable seven-figure salary and bonuses. After pleading guilty, Levine cooperated with the government's investigation, and others were charged.

Since the foundation of Wall Street's business is trust, client confidence, needless to say, was shaken. But all this was a mere rumble compared to the earthquake that soon followed. Most people on Wall Street assume that information leaks from time to time; some even claim it's epidemic. Yet almost no one was prepared when the next person accused was someone of such power and prominence—Ivan Boesky, an extremely successful arbitrageur known even outside the strict confines of the Wall Street community. The idea that Boesky had made his millions not by talent alone but with the aid of inside information seemed like absolute treason. Boesky, who like Levine agreed to cooperate, paid a whopping $100 million fine for his crimes and still went to jail. It was the biggest insider trading case in history, and just the tip of the iceberg.

Not all tip-passing is as conscious and businesslike as Dennis Levine's and Ivan Boesky's. Just think how hard it is to keep a secret, particularly a juicy one. Just think how easy it would be to let a little something slip over drinks. Remember the movie *The Big Chill?* When Kevin Kline and William Hurt are out jogging, Kline lets drop that his company, Running Dog, is about to be acquired, and that if Hurt hurries and buys stock, he'll make a lot of money. A tip between friends? Sure. Innocent? Maybe. Legal? No.

In an effort to gain tighter controls, leading firms have taken some serious steps. Some have installed sophisticated locks, started to rely on electronic rather than paper lists of confidential items, and begun shredding more documents. They've given stern talks to their staffs about ethics and penalties. But even more, they've started paying closer attention to whom they're hiring. Having solid credentials is no longer enough; you also have to inspire trust. Because a firm that cannot be trusted is a firm that will lose its clients, and afterall, who if not the employees constitutes a firm?

When respected economist Henry Kaufman was asked if he thought the ethics of the financial community have, in general, been compromised, he responded: "I would hope not. It's very difficult for me to make that judgment. I think it's important that the ethics of the financial markets are not compromised. Financial markets are very unusual for many reasons, but one of them is the very fact that transactions in large amounts are consummated over the telephone, without a written contract, without legal documentation. Ninety-nine and nine-tenths percent of the time there are no ifs or buts about that oral agreement. It's an extraordinary thing. We trade hundreds of millions of dollars; one institution calls up and says, 'We want to sell you $50 million or $20 million,' and we say we'll buy at a certain price, and that's it. That really reflects a high degree of morality and standards, and a high degree of trust.

"I think the problem at times can be that in this tremendous fury of trading and volatility, people tend to forget what the underlying transaction is all about. [They just think of] prices going up or prices going down. Underlying these transactions is the financing of some state and local government or a business or a household, helping institutions increase their liquidity in order to meet some demand on them, and so on. These are very important and essential functions that tend to be forgotten in the fury of a day, and it's incumbent on senior management all over Wall Street and in financial institutions to remind their operating groups that that's what the nature of the business is. Occasionally that is forgotten."

Senator John D. Dingell of Michigan wrote in the *New York Times,* "I have always believed that the securities industry is vital to the growth of our economy. America's free capital markets and open democratic government go hand in hand—with both based on trust." In both arenas—Wall Street and Washington—that trust has been tested in recent years.

Yet, the faith holds, business continues, and young men and women with a true desire to contribute to this country's economic well-being and to meet their own professional goals are flocking in record numbers to the Street of Dreams. Are you one of them? Where will you best fit in? Read on and find out.

PART TWO

THE
PLAYERS

CHAPTER 3

INVESTMENT BANKERS: THE GENTLEMEN OF BANKING

Once upon a time, not very long ago, the world of investment banking was a bastion of exclusivity, a private club, you might say, of America's well-heeled, well-placed old guard. What placed that heel on the welcome mat of high finance was a fortuitous compendium of "rights": being born with the "right" family name, having gone to the "right" schools, being part of the "right" social set. In other words, connections meant everything. They not only got you started but kept you going behind the polished doors of Wall Street's elite firms. Once professional relationships were built they were not easily torn down. Now all that has changed. As *Business Week* noted in an article called "Power on Wall Street" (July 7, 1986), "On Wall Street today, profit is power. But until recently, power was pedigree."

This is good news for those whose American Dream is pillowed in the world of investment banking. The polished doors of investment banking have opened to anyone with the intelligence and drive to make it. Harold Tanner, who as former managing director of corporate finance at Salomon Brothers was an active recruiter of young talent for that firm, notes some of the ways in which investment banking has changed since its gentleman banker days. "Thirty years ago if you had an account you had an account. Today it's the best idea; its the quickest call; it's the most creativity; it's the best execution. It's also a good relationship. You can't do it without a good relationship. But you can't do it on good relationships alone. If you can't execute, the relationship isn't worth anything. If you can execute, the relationship gives you the opportunity to complete the transaction."

And once the transaction is completed, will a grateful client come back for the next deal? Perhaps, but probably not out of gratitude or loyalty. More likely, it will depend on who comes up with the best idea, the quickest call, the most creativity. Investment banking earnings depend on whether a firm can perform a specific task, not on whom the firm was cozy with last year or even last month. Long-term is no longer a viable phrase in this context because business is business. The solid world of the gentleman banker has largely gone the way of the manual typewriter: a quaint example of how things were once done.

THE NEW INVESTMENT BANKER

Investment banking has become a triple-A glamour job, and it's a profession many ambitious young people are heading for with the speed of light. Power and money have always had their allure, and never more so than now, when conservative suits and highly polished shoes suddenly seem as heart-stopping as a rock star's leather pants. Such pulse-taking publications as *M* and *Rolling Stone* have found today's new investment bankers newsworthy enough to feature in full-length articles. These magazines have dubbed them "The Baby Bankers" and "The Brat Bankers," noting that their ambition and work pace are overshadowed only by their enormous incomes. But more on these details in a minute.

Investment banking has become a young person's field. Harold Tanner points out that out of 100 managing directors at Salomon Brothers, only 10 to 12 are over age fifty. In Salomon's corporate finance area, 65 percent are under thirty-five. As for recent graduates, fully 400 of Yale's 1986 class of 1,250 applied for analyst positions at First Boston alone. Harvard's MBAs aren't waiting for the grass to grow either. When Harold Tanner received his MBA from Harvard in 1956, only two of his classmates, he points out, were hired by Goldman, Sachs. Compare this with the thirty-two MBAs Goldman, Sachs swept into its ranks in 1986. They, along with the best and the brightest from colleges and universities all across the country, are beating a path to the money and power that the financial world offers. What this means, of course, is massive competition for top jobs. At First Boston 4,000 resumes were picked through before 100 offers were made for 70 spots. But competition *can* be beaten by those who know the rules of the game.

WHAT IS INVESTMENT BANKING, ANYWAY?

Before we cover what it's like to work in investment banking and what it takes to get there, let's discuss for a minute what investment bankers do.

Because investment bankers work to help corporations grow and move forward, they are seen as being in a service industry. Traditionally, the main role of the investment banker has been one of advisor to and matchmaker between those who need money and those who have it. IBs take private companies public when they need to raise capital, and raise capital for public companies by putting together packages of stocks and bonds to sell to the public.

While traditional underwriting is still a major part of investment banking, the explosion of new products, as well as the surge in mergers and acquisitions (M & A), has radically changed investment banking's staid face. Today some of the added roles of IBs include offering financial advice on takeovers, advising governments and foreign countries, managing pension and money funds, and trading securities.

Within the now-broad category of investment banking, there are many directions for you to take. Some people specialize in particular types of business, such as M & A or private placements or currency swaps. Others concentrate on a particular area, such as the energy field or health care or utilities. Still others remain generalists, preferring to work with a variety of clients on different types of transactions. Your ability to choose how you want to work depends on the opportunities your firm offers, on the state and activity levels of the markets, and on your personality and talents.

THE HOT SPOTS

Currently, we're going through a phase when mergers and acquisitions is a red-hot area, so hot in fact that Lazard Frères' Felix Rohatyn, one of the most illustrious investment bankers (he was a head sorcerer in the successful plan to save New York City from bankruptcy a couple of years ago) and mastermind of megadollar deals, is so concerned about the weakening of both the economy and industry due to takeovers and mergers that he issued a serious warning: " . . . Things are getting badly out of hand. . . . The way we are going will destroy all of us in this business. Someday there is going to be a major recession, major scandals. All of us may be sitting in front of congressional committees trying to explain what we were doing." How right Mr. Rohatyn was! The end of 1986 brought the shattering news of serious trading misconduct, and in 1987 the net widened. The exposure of foul play has upset and might yet alter Wall Street's practices.

Nevertheless, one thing remains unchanged as the top guns continue to drive deal after deal into place: They are making tons of money. And the demand for young talent is tremendous as the M & A pot begins to boil. To give you an idea of the current boom, between 1969 and 1981, there were twelve $1 billion-plus mergers; between 1981 and 1984, there were forty-five. But in 1985 and 1986, the figures soared to twenty-six and thirty-one, respectively. While the deals are less predictable than many and the tone is often uncomfortably adversarial, the power and financial rewards that go with the territory are extremely alluring.

What exactly is mergers and acquisitions? The simplest definition says it's when one company buys another. The investment banker acts something like a real estate agent, putting the deal together and taking a percentage. Of course, it's all much more complicated than selling a house, but that's the basic idea.

One of the bigger deals in recent history was Philip Morris's buyout of General Foods for a whopping $5.7 billion. The cut for the three investment banks who put it all together: $24.3 million. Not bad. And you can be sure that a healthy piece of that pie was served to the individuals responsible for putting the Maxwell House coffee cup into the Marlboro man's hands.

Mergers and takeovers frequently leave companies in disarray, with loyal employees having unceremoniously been booted out. This is one criticism of the practice that you'll hear. Yet some deals taste very sweet to the deposed corporate kings. For Michel Bergerac, former chairman of Revlon, for example, losing his job was probably the most lucrative deal of his life. When Pantry Pride got control of Revlon in November 1986, Bergerac resigned, walking away with somewhere in the neighborhood of $35 million in cash, stocks, and stock options. Arrangements of this ilk, known as golden parachutes, certainly ensure a soft landing for those who were once at the top.

But not all trees bear fruit, and long worked-on deals sometimes don't pan out. In the ongoing war for cola dominance, Coke and Pepsi have made quite an effort to gain control of surrounding markets—but not without seeing some of their bubbles burst. PepsiCo's June 1986 efforts to acquire Seven-Up Co.'s domestic business collapsed against opposition from the

Federal Trade Commission. And in a fair-is-fair reversal, the Federal Trade Commission stepped in again when Coke went after Dr. Pepper. No way, they said, no doubt disappointing more than a few dealmakers.

The flip side of the takeover is the once obscure transaction known as the leveraged buyout, where corporate officers turn publicly held firms into private businesses, often to escape the clutches of corporate raiders. Here's another hot area, because the success rate is incredibly high, and lots of people see action. Bankers, institutional investors, firms that specialize in buyouts, and the managers of acquired companies all get involved.

WHAT IT TAKES AND WHAT YOU CAN MAKE

"Many are called, but few are chosen" has never been more apt. The competition for investment banking positions is fierce, with literally thousands of applicants applying to a top firm for a few dozen spots. To make the final cut, you have to be good and you have to prove it—fast. But there's no use in even trying out for the team if you don't possess the following traits:

Serious Ambition. Once you begin working as an investment banker, you can pretty much forget about the rest of your life. This is an all-consuming field that demands your full devotion, and you have to be willing to forgo social life, family life, and love life in favor of professional life. Many young IBs feel the trade-off is more than worth the price. As one twenty-six-year-old on the fast track observes, "I have more money in the bank than I know what to do with, and no time to do anything with it if I knew. But having financial security definitely is better than not having it, and someday when I do have time the money will be there for me to enjoy." Other IBs stress that it's not just the financial rewards that make working so hard worth it. They love the challenges and they love being close to the seat of power.

They're more than willing to delay dating, marriage, family, traveling, sports and cultural events, and life's other pleasures in favor of the rush they get at their jobs. When thinking about whether investment banking is for you, remember that without that single-minded determination to "go for the burn," you'll have difficulty sticking out the extraordinary demands. You can't just *think* you want this life, you really do have to want it.

Stamina. A slow work week will gobble only sixty hours of your time. A normal week will run about eighty hours, and 100-hour weeks are certainly within the realm of possibility, particularly when a deal is peaking. Stories of all-nighters are common, complete with dashes to the home front for a quick shower and change of clothes before heading back to the office for another full day. Typically, an IB will arrive at work between 7:30 and 8:00 and stay as late as necessary, often past midnight. Six-day workweeks are the norm; seven-day weeks not unusual. Business travel is frequent and often called for on short notice. If you do manage a bit of vacation time, it's recommended that you flee to Katmandu or some other spot where you're totally unreachable, because, young IBs note, if the office can beep you, they will. No wonder investment banking is becoming more and more a young person's profession. It takes the energy of youth to keep up such a grueling pace.

Personality. Recruiters talk about the "fit" of an applicant with a firm. What they mean is that certain types slide more easily into place at certain firms than at others. It helps to know the personalities of the various firms (and each does have a personality), though this isn't particularly easy information to get. What clearly wins points at any interview are the following personality adjectives: *quick, energetic, sharp, witty, charming, confident, well-rounded, focused, determined, flexible, creative.* With these traits your chances not only of being hired but also of being successful on the job are greatly enhanced.

What You Get For What You Give. Quite a lot. Figures
vary, but even the lowest is none too shabby. Analysts—these
are recent college graduates for whom this is a first "grown-up"
job—can expect to start in the area of $27,000 to $30,000.
Increases and second-year bonuses easily raise that figure to
$50,000. MBAs start more at the $60,000 to $80,000 mark,
topping $100,000 by the end of the first year. It's not unusual
for a person in his late twenties to be raking in $250,000, and
incomes in the high six figures are not unheard of. Neither are
millionaire thirty-year-olds.

BREAKING IN

There are three main ways to break into investment banking: (1)
liberal arts undergraduates come in as two-year research analysts; (2) MBAs enter after receiving their degrees; and (3)
people with legal, management consulting, or accounting backgrounds make career switches to Wall Street.

Recruiting is the word undergraduates and MBAs want to
remember because that's how banks, brokerage houses, and
other large Wall Street businesses find the talent they seek.
Where do they look? Mostly on campuses across the country,
particularly at the top schools. The colleges mentioned again and
again include Harvard, Princeton, Stanford, the Wharton School
of the University of Pennsylvania, MIT, Columbia, Northwest-
ern, and Dartmouth, though these certainly are not the only
schools earmarked by recruiters.

What happens during the recruiting process is that represen-
tatives from firms visit campuses. Some offer sessions to any
student who signs up; during these sessions, presentations are
made, perhaps a film is shown, and students have an opportunity
to introduce themselves. Other firms conduct closed interviews
with promising students who have submitted their resumes
beforehand. Either way, it goes without saying that attending a

school where major firms recruit dramatically enhances your chances of landing a fast-track job.

If you don't attend a school where firms recruit, you're not completely cut out of the picture; you just have to find the firms instead of letting them find you. This can be accomplished by researching which firms interest you and to whom you should send your resume. Then you have to do the best job possible of selling yourself, including showing terrific initiative and tapping any contacts you may have.

Summer job programs are also a popular way for Wall Street to meet its newest stars. From the firms' point of view, observing someone for three months gives them the opportunity to rate the candidates' job performance and test how they might work out on a full-time basis once they graduate. The student employees also get to test the waters, particularly if they try a different firm each summer.

Wall Street's need for talented young people has grown astronomically as the business has gotten more complex. Because growth has occurred so rapidly, some of the recruiting practices and available information haven't kept pace. During the recruiting process, a candidate can distinguish himself by showing he's put a lot of effort into getting elusive bottom-line information about the investment banking world. One recruiter for a major investment bank suggests that it's precisely this lack of available information that acts as a built-in screening device, because it immediately separates the dabblers from those who are truly interested. "Being able to distinguish between the thousands of bright, articulate people out there is very difficult," he says. "So interest and knowledge of the Street is one method we use to evaluate."

The recruiter also stresses the importance of sheer chemistry. "The recruiting process," he notes, "is almost entirely a series of one-on-one interviews, and any time a process is dominated by that type of procedure, the chemistry between two people has a lot to do with their success or failure. One of the

hardest things in the recruiting process for candidates to understand is the different personalities of the different firms, to
understand where they ultimately would be most comfortable
and where they would fit in the best."

As for attorneys, some are making the leap from law firm to
investment house, or even directly from law school to the
Street. When law firms visit Yale for their annual October recruiting fest, for example, they now compete with such powerful
investment banks as Salomon Brothers and Goldman, Sachs.
Again, young professionals find the money a big draw. Attorneys
report having jumped from $80,000 to over $200,000 a year by
making the switch. Yet many also claim that they want Wall
Street simply because it's more fun. Says one lawyer who went
from a large law firm to a large brokerage house, "At the law
firm, I watched our banking clients put together the creative
part of the deal, while I was stuck with the technical stuff. It was
clear to me that bankers were at the center of the action; I
wanted to be there, too."

THE RESEARCH ANALYST PROGRAM

The concept of a programmed approach to learning how to be
a securities analyst is a relatively new trend in investment banking, but one that's growing by leaps and bounds. For those who
can get into a research analyst program (they're highly competitive), it's a great opportunity to experience investment banking
from the inside track.

Research analyst programs, mostly operated at the big New
York firms, are geared to those with undergraduate degrees.
Recent grads are invited to spend two years at an investment
bank before moving into an MBA program for that all-important
degree. During those two years, the analyst works extremely
hard, figures out if this is the life for him or her, makes excellent
money, and leaves an impression—hopefully positive—with the

firm. The firm hopes each analyst will work out ideally, taking back to campus love stories about the bank, and returning, MBA in hand, to work loyally unto retirement.

Sometimes everyone's dreams come true, and sometimes they don't. But there's no denying that for recent grads, a research analyst position is a terrific way to test the investment banking waters. Plus there's another benefit, and quite a big one at that. More and more MBA programs want their students to enter with about two years of solid work experience under their belts. To be able to write on an application that you're coming from an analyst program does wonders for your chances for admission. Also, since analyst programs are set, two-year positions, no employer is annoyed when you quit to go back to school. On the contrary, it's what they anticipate.

To back up just a bit, does your undergraduate major matter when applying for an analyst position? Yes and no. English, history, philosophy, and music majors have been known to be plucked up by the likes of Salomon and First Boston, and in fact some recruiters prefer liberal arts majors. But often, someone with some quantitative orientation and knowledge of business, economics, and accounting has the best chance of a job offer.

For more about the research analyst program, see chapter 12.

NEED AN MBA?

Yes, yes, and decidedly yes. To be an investment banker, you're going to need a masters in business administration. The only exception may be attorneys and other professionals who come into the field with impressive degrees and work experience. For the rest of us, however, those three little letters are the magic mantra that opens the big-deal doors.

Opinions do differ on how single-minded you should be about

pursuing a business education. Some people believe that there is no time to lose, and the best path is the most direct one. They suggest that you load up on courses that are obviously useful. Why fool around with philosophy and English literature? What good could they possibly do?

But many other professionals advise students to concentrate on getting a broader education at the undergraduate level, and then focus on such courses as economics and accounting in graduate school. William C. Nelson, of First RepublicBank Corporation in Dallas, sums up this valid point of view: "I feel very strongly that a liberal education is the best grounding for a career in banking, because you have to organize your thoughts; you have to be able to talk; you have to be able to relate well to people. You are using psychology, salesmanship, debating skills—things you'll never learn in accounting class. If you spend all your time in accounting and economics classes, you will miss a lot of the basic grounding that's extremely valuable in a banking career." Nelson and others recommend that you get your undergraduate degree in liberal arts, and then move on for an MBA.

William C. Nelson

A JOB DESCRIPTION

Even as you envision leading the light brigade into multibillion dollar deals, you probably have this nagging feeling that this is not precisely what you'll get to do until you pay some dues. And that's exactly right. Research analysts and even freshly minted MBAs are grunts in the investment banking army. Despite the fancy salaries, their work by and large is about as engaging as that of a private who's made to peel potatoes.

Typically, they work on a three- to four-person team, organized by project. A person can work on several projects simultaneously. And what does the junior member of the team do?

First of all, there is numbers crunching, lots and lots of numbers crunching—analyzing a company, its position relative to the industry, the financial statements, the accounting records, looking at the markets, whether it be for a merger or an acquisition, and helping determine the price; in a debt offering, it's figuring out at what interest-rate level the company ought to be able to issue debt, and on and on until this analytical work supports the contemplated transaction.

Then there is secretarial work. That's right, secretarial, such as heavy doses of proofreading the documents for the transactions and standing at the Xerox machine literally all night. For this America's best and brightest are scampering to Wall Street?

You bet they are. Because this is how investment bankers learn the business, from the bottom up, you might say— by working on transactions, asking questions, and staying alert.

Within two to three years, junior team members move up to the middle rung. Here they hone delegating skills and get to think about the big picture—where the transaction needs to be directed and how they're going to get it there.

KATHERINE UPDIKE:
ON BEING AN INVESTMENT BANKER IN A
COMMERCIAL BANK IN CHICAGO

Katherine Updike heads Chase Manhattan Bank's Chicago investment banking division. There are several things that make
this a situation worth examining. First of all, because Chase is
a commercial bank and therefore is barred through the Glass–
Steagall Act from underwriting, it may not be the first place
someone might think to look for a job. Second, because of their
geographic location, Updike and her colleagues tend to respond to
the needs of a very specific kind of client.

Updike is not bothered in the least by the restrictions of the
Glass–Steagall Act. She believes that one of the most significant
things that's happening today is the way deregulation is changing
the "complexion" of the banking industry. "I don't think that
entering into an investment bank to be an investment banker is
any longer the most obvious choice," she says. "You may find
opportunities to be much greater in the banks that are developing
and have the momentum as they build their M & A staffs, their
private placement staffs, their corporate finance advisory staffs."

In fact, Updike points to opportunities in commercial banks as a key trend for investment bankers. She reasons that as investment banking inevitably relies more heavily on a capital base, the commercial banks, rather than the investment banks, are where that capital will be found. Expansion, then, is likely to come from those banks with the largest capital bases.

Updike also points out that although Glass–Steagall prohibits commercial banks from underwriting, other traditional investment firm activities—such as mergers and acquisitions, private placement of debt securities, and rate arbitrage—are now being done on a regular basis by commercial banks. And, of course, commercial banks can and do underwrite outside of the U.S., with the exception of Japan where it is also prohibited.

As for what Updike does for her clients, she describes it as a combination of corporate finance and corporate finance advising. "What we're trying to do is integrate the traditional banking and investment banking decisions in a company. By investments I mean making a senior debt loan to a company, using the capabilities of our investment bank." She also helps indentify both market-driven and customer-driven opportunities; then she brings the bank's resources to her customers.

Rather than aim their business at Fortune 100 or 200 companies, Updike and her colleagues go for the upper middle market, where the competition is less intense and the need for good advisory services is great. Her typical client might be a food service company or a medical technology company with a sales size of 100 to 500. This company may be public or private, but it probably won't have broad distribution and won't be in the public debt market.

In Katherine Updike's current position, she may never be part of one of those well-publicized deals where one multinational corporation eats up another. But that's probably just fine with her. By all appearances, she is quite gratified and stimulated by the work she does.

MIKE MILKEN,
SENIOR EXECUTIVE VICE PRESIDENT,
DREXEL BURNHAM LAMBERT

At Drexel Burnham Lambert, there are three names to know: Frederick Joseph, Robert Linton, and Mike Milken. Joseph is the giant investment bank's president and CEO, Linton is its chairman, and Milken . . . well, Milken officially is a rather modest senior executive vice president. So why is his a name to remember? Read on.

At forty-one, Mike Milken has been described as a wizard, a creative genius, and a mystical figure, and these accolades are not newly earned. Milken's been at his trade for a good number of years. In his younger days, he was often called a wunderkind. More recently, he's been compared to J. P. Morgan, because like that turn-of-the-century industrial baron, Milken is a particularly aggressive power player who has reshaped the financial world. What Milken has built his substantial career on, in the process making quite a handsome purse for himself and Drexel Burnham, is a queasy-sounding item known as junk bonds. Quite simply, junk bonds are investments in high-yielding, below investment-grade corporate debt securities. Not quite so simple are the ways in which Milken maneuvers junk bonds. Suffice it to say that he does so with such extraordinary skill that veterans of the investment wars are dazzled.

Moving right down to the bottom line, Milken's junk bond sales and trading group may be responsible for as much as fifty percent of Drexel Burnham's total revenues. The firm is privately held, so figures like this are not publicly available. Still, it is thought that Drexel pulled profits of $350 million for the first six months of 1986, up from $450 million for all of 1985. For his substantial assistance in this startling growth, Milken likely earned around $40 million in 1985, a figure that may have at least doubled in 1986. While no one knows exactly what the Wizard of Wall Street *makes, he is surely one of the wealthiest people in the business.*

As for Mike Milken the man, his reputation as an intensely private workaholic remains intact. It was in 1978 that Milken got permission from Drexel's higher-ups to move himself and his operations to Beverly Hills. He wanted, he said, to extend his workday, to be near his aging father, and to have more time for his family. Those desires have hardly stopped him from working hard. By all reports, Milken puts in fourteen- to eighteen-hour days, plays tennis with his paper-stuffed attache case close by, and lives in a relatively simple manner. He usually arrives at the trading room at 4:30 A.M. and stays until at least 7:30 P.M. Three assistants work in relays to keep up with him.

Even while this powerhouse, creator of the multibillion-dollar junk bond market, continues to carve his career as the leading financier of our time and one of the most powerful, behind-the-scenes men in America, he is, as of this writing, being closely watched in connection with the insider trading scandals. Whatever the outcome of this, Mike Milken has already made his mark on the financial world . . . and things will never be the same.

CHAPTER 4

BROKERS: STEADY
AS IT GOES

Someone is looking at his hard-earned savings and thinking to himself, "I bet I could make some money with this money. You know, buy stocks or bonds or maybe even play the futures market." Someone else needs an IRA or Keogh and wonders if a special fund will give her a better return than a commercial bank. A third person has a specific goal—maybe to get enough cash for a downpayment on a house—and he's not sure how to meet that goal.

Meet L. Kirk Payne, vice president, investments, PaineWebber; Scott Randall, financial consultant at Shearson/Lehman Brothers; and Carole Delmoni, associate vice president, Investments, with Prudential-Bache Securities. All three, despite differences in titles, are stockbrokers covering the retail trade. Their job is to help individuals (not IBM or NYU or any other institution) meet their investment objectives. Their clients are doctors, lawyers, small business owners, anyone who has capital to invest and needs an expert to advise him, place the orders, and carefully watch the ups and downs of those investments. In that way, retail brokers are quite different from most people in the financial field, where so much emphasis is placed on the big bucks from the big-time institutional spenders.

As Kirk Payne points out: "Transactions and relationships can range from one trade only—helping somebody sell a couple of hundred shares of stock or buy a bond—to helping manage an entire portfolio." Yet before getting involved in actually managing a portfolio, Payne says, most brokers insist that the client have at least $50,000 to invest, though a $100,000 minimum requirement is not atypical these days. Scott Randall and Carole Delmoni both agree with the $50,000 to $100,000 minimum figure. All three brokers, however, stress that there are no hard and fast rules about this. It depends entirely on the individual broker and his or her desire to work with a particular client.

There are also brokers for institutions—corporations, insurance companies, pension funds, and the like—and not surprisingly, they are called institutional salespeople. Institutional salespeople tend to differ from retail brokers in that they usually handle fewer transactions, but for much larger amounts (think about how much more money an insurance company has to invest than, say, the owners of a mom-and-pop grocery). The size and complexity of these transactions is such that institutional salespeople also tend to become quite specialized, handling specific types of investments such as institutional equity stocks or specific types of clients, pension funds only, for example. The exciting thing about this end of the business is that it's the institutions, not individuals, that move hundreds of thousands of shares in and out of positions and by doing so create the market's underlying momentum. While the public's action is a mere drop in the bucket, the institutions rule the tides.

HOW THESE THREE BROKE IN

Three different people, three different career paths to the same job. All are extremely successful and satisfied with their chosen profession. Here are their stories:

By all accounts, L. Kirk Payne should have become an investment banker. Certainly the choice was his to make. Payne comes from the "right" background and went to the "right"

Clockwise from top: L. Kirk Payne, Carole Delmoni,
Scott Randall

schools—Yale undergraduate and Columbia Business School.
Unlike many brokers, he has an MBA. What's more, nineteen
years ago, when he went into the business, retail brokers were
considered to be less than the cream of the crop. But Payne,
imposingly tall and sophisticated yet always affable, suspected
that managing money would be more fun than making deals. And
so it has been. Payne went against tradition and entered what
has been for him the best of all possible jobs: working directly
with individuals who need his expertise.

Scott Randall grew up in the Midwest, and it's his roots that keep him there. Working out of Cincinnati's Shearson/Lehman Brothers office, his clients tend to be the hardworking, generally conservative folk of German heritage who settled in that city long ago. Randall, believes (as does Kirk Payne) that it's best to develop clients whose values and tendencies are somewhat close to your own. That way, he says, everyone is more comfortable and communication is easier. (Payne tells how one Boston broker built up a very good clientele of Maine potato farmers by driving right up to their doors on weekends and vacations, introducing himself, and making his pitch.) Randall recognizes that "for someone who is extremely aggressive and wants to really beat the fast path, New York is probably one of the best places to do that." But for him, Cincinnati is home, and it's there that he's carving out his niche in "one of the nicest" thirty-broker offices in the country. As for income differences between being in the Big City and somewhere farther out, Randall doesn't equate location with prosperity. "It might take longer to establish yourself," he says, but Cincinnati still has people who need the services he offers. "It doesn't matter where you are. If you work hard, you will do well."

Carole Delmoni sees the business from a different perspective. She remembers well how in the 1960s, "Wall Street closed the door to women." This was tough for Delmoni, who had a natural interest in the market. Even before she was old enough to work, she'd read the financial pages, and it wasn't long after she started making money of her own that she invested in the stock market. After Delmoni graduated from Brooklyn College with a degree in psychology, she accepted a job as assistant to an institutional broker at a small brokerage firm. Although it wasn't likely in 1968 that she could go on to become a broker herself, she received her license that year and used it to handle accounts and take orders for her boss. By the mid-1970s, there were more opportunities, and Delmoni decided to strike out on her own. Her first position as a full-time broker was at Merrill Lynch. In 1981, she joined Prudential-Bache, where she is today.

BREAKING IN

As in every corner of Wall Street, an MBA is useful to a stock-broker. However, it is not essential. Here's what is: sales experience. A broker's job is a sales job, only more so. As Kirk Payne points out, the biggest difference between this sales job and others is that whereas in a typical sales job you are working solely for a company and the product they sell, as a broker, you have to work as much for your clients as for the firm. "You really have two sets of people you're answering to," Payne says. "Only if you please your clients will you get referrals, by far the best way to expand a client list." Certainly every salesperson has to please the buyers, but here it's absolutely crucial to focus on what your clients want and need, rather than foisting the company's products on them. These are ongoing relationships, and you want them to last.

Because the sales situation is such a delicate one, no firm is likely to be thrilled to get a new college grad who hasn't any work experience under his or her belt. It really doesn't matter what it is you have sold; what counts is a demonstrated ability to sell. A couple of years are all that's needed. So if you graduated from college at twenty-two and have worked in sales for three to five years, you are, at twenty-five or twenty-six or twenty-seven, in the best position to switch to the brokerage field. Some brokers report that a college diploma isn't even necessary, if you have strong verbal skills, a neat appearance, and can demonstrate intelligence. These qualities, teamed with sales experience, may be enough to give you the break you're looking for.

When you decide to become a broker, you'll apply to firms as for any other job, with a resumé and perhaps an application form. You'll likely be asked at the interview, among other questions, about your sales experience and how you functioned as a salesperson. What was your record as a salesperson? Did you enjoy talking to people? How did you deal with rejection? How well did you understand your product and how important was this to you?

Once you're hired, you'll face a battery of certification tests. The exams qualify you to work at the New York Stock Exchange as a registered representative. Plus you have to pass the National Association of Securities Dealers (NASD) test. You'll probably want a commodities license and perhaps an insurance license, and that means more tests. Your firm, who after all has a vested interest in seeing you pass with flying colors, will help you by providing study materials and possibly a course. The branch manager will lend moral and professional support. Then, when you're certified, the company will probably send you through a training program (these can vary from a few hours to several months) to teach you specifics, such as how to open an account and conduct special sales. Finally, after all this, you'll be a full-fledged broker and on your way.

A DESK, A PHONE, AND OUR BEST WISHES

What's appealing to many people who become brokers, Kirk Payne accurately notes, is that even though you work for a firm, you are developing your own business, and you can set it up any way you want. Your work methods and hours are up to you. Sleep till noon and work till 3 A.M., if that's the way you like to do it. Keep your ear glued to the phone all day long, or like the broker who wooed the Maine potato farmers, take your sales technique right to people's homes. As long as you do the business you're expected to do, how and when you do it is of no consequence.

But there lies the rub. "As long as you do the business . . . " As always in the financial world, the bottom line reigns supreme, which in this case means building a client list. That's a tall order; it doesn't happen overnight. Once you're a fully licensed broker, what you get from the firm, according to Payne, is "a desk, a phone, and our best wishes." Actually, you do get a bit more than that: computers, secretarial help, and product and research backup, for example.

You might also get a modest salary, but as time goes by, that salary is reduced, not increased, until you're floating on your own, making your living from client commissions. "We don't want you to be comfortable," admits one branch manager. "We're looking for self-starters. The salary we give is like a pair of water wings; you'd better learn to swim before we take them away."

So how do you go about learning to swim? Mostly with a phone clamped in your hand. You rack your brain for whatever contacts you may have—friends of the family, current and former neighbors, even professionals, like doctors and dentists, you've gone to over the years. You ask other people for their contacts. And you make cold calls to people you've never met, lots and lots of cold calls. You comb the phone book and dial and talk and maybe get hung up on, and maybe get a client. Carole Delmoni remembers how hard it was getting started. "It was a lot of work as far as developing business was concerned. I actually had to prove to the clients that I was working for them." Scott Randall hasn't forgotten those early days either. "You have to be able to present yourself as competent," he says. "The average length of time from when you start talking to somebody to when you open an account is about three months." That in itself can be frustrating and a little frightening.

Plus the competition is fierce. Not only are there thousands of brokers vying for the same client base, but aspects of the business have changed in recent years. Although they used to be set, commissions are now negotiable. Banks now offer brokerage services, and discount brokers, like Charles Schwab & Company and Quick & Reilly Inc., which provide no-frills brokerage services, have sprung up. For brokers just building their careers, it's a long, hard climb, but the rewards and the professional satisfaction, as Kirk Payne, Carole Delmoni, and Scott Randall know, are definitely worth the effort.

THE REWARDS

In addition to having the satisfaction of helping individuals make sound decisions and meet their financial goals, successful brokers (and no broker stays in business for long if he or she doesn't make the leap to success) earn an excellent income.

Different firms work in different ways, but generally, this is a commission business. Income may be paid out as a draw against commissions, or you may get a salary based on production, meaning past performance. But any way it's packaged, what you're finally getting is based on your level of productivity, so the pressure is on to do business.

How much does the firm expect its brokers to produce? Most brokerage houses will want to see the broker get up to a minimum of $200,000 annually in gross commissions. Obviously this doesn't happen on Day One; you start low and work your way up. Still, the expectation is there. The broker can expect to take home about 40 percent of the gross commission. The other 60 percent goes to the firm. Therefore, if a broker has pulled in $200,000, he'll make $80,000 for himself. At some firms, the most productive brokers get a slightly higher commission. Whereas heel-draggers who bring in only $150,000 in gross commissions after four years on the job may find their commissions cut back to 25 percent or 30 percent. As for the upper rung, there are million-dollar producers around, go-getters who see $450,000 or more annually for themselves. Actually, there is no ceiling to what a stockbroker can earn; this is a sky's the limit business. The highest-paid brokers at Merrill Lynch earned a hefty $2 million each in 1985. Still, a broker who makes $450,-000 a year is considered to be doing very well.

SO WHAT DO YOU DO IN THIS JOB?

You work incredibly hard to get a client list in shape; that much we've established. And it's pretty clear that the job entails buying and selling stocks, bonds, and other financial instruments for your clients. Okay. But those are the bricks. Now for the mortar that holds the building in place. This is the personal part of the business, the part that's about really caring for your clients and providing them with the best service you can offer.

Finding out your clients' needs and building trust are the first steps. Scott Randall prefers meeting his clients face to face to do detailed financial planning. He asks questions like, "Where is your money now? What investments do you currently have? What are you trying to achieve?" He'll find out their tax bracket and whether they need tax shelters. Are they interested in income or growth? What is their financial situation vis-à-vis their children? Have they settled their estate yet? Only then can he make sound recommendations on how they might proceed. "The more you know, the better equipped you are to do the best job you can for your clients," he says. For Kirk Payne, this kind of service is what differentiates the work he does from that of a discount broker (see below), or, for that matter, from any other Joe on the job. If you don't know or aren't responding to your clients' needs, you can't help them meet their objectives. And if you don't have your clients' confidence, they won't stick with you for long . . . or refer other clients, which is how many brokers build up their business. So it is definitely in your best interest to give them the time they need, and not only in the beginning, because nothing is static—the market shifts; clients' objectives change, all kinds of things happen. You have to be ready, willing, and able to move flexibly on behalf of your clients, and that means knowing what they want.

The other thing you have to keep up with is the business itself. With so many financial instruments being introduced all the time and with the industry as a whole changing so rapidly (not to mention the new tax laws), it's important that you stay on top of things. It's the only way you're going to know when to get in or out of an investment and what to offer your clients. Scott Randall realizes that if all he had to work with were stocks, there'd be periods when he'd go broke. Luckily, there are 300, 400, or more kinds of investments to choose from—everything from box cars to helicopters to movies. It's crucial that you keep up-to-date.

A QUICK WORD ON DISCOUNT BROKERAGE

In recent years a new breed of brokers has appeared on the scene: discount brokers. These guys are the no-frills version of the business. They provide quick, basic service for a lower commission than traditional brokers, and they're great for people who know exactly what they need and want. Fast and to the point, they include such companies as Charles Schwab & Company, headquartered in San Francisco and one of the largest discount brokerage firms, New York's Quick & Reilly Inc., and C. D. Anderson & Company, also located in San Francisco. Fidelity and Dreyfus also offer discount stock brokerage services to complement their stable of mutual fund offerings. If heavy-duty service and customer involvement aren't your strong suits but you like the nuts and bolts of buy/sell, you may find working as a discount broker just the game for you.

WHO'S WHO, WHAT'S WHAT, AND HOW MUCH

Lest you still fear that New York is the only place to be, the vast number of regional offices most firms have should reassure you that your options are many. The April 1987 issue of *Institutional Investor* printed a comprehensive listing of America's 100 biggest brokers. Here is an extract of the top fifteen. (This list was published before Shearson/Lehman Brothers and E. F. Hutton merged.)

	NAME OF FIRM	TOTAL CAPITAL ($ MILLIONS)	NUMBER OF EMPLOYEES	NUMBER OF OFFICES	# OF REGISTERED REPS
1.	Salomon Brothers	$3,209.2	5,383	8	1,139
2.	Shearson Lehman Brothers	3,122.0	25,004	336	6,053
3.	Merrill Lynch, Pierce, Fenner & Smith	2,864.8	34,520	481	11,062
4.	Goldman, Sachs & Co.	1,951.0	6,049	16	1,377
5.	Drexel Burnham Lambert	1,870.5	10,172	62	2,171
6.	First Boston Corp.	1,363.8	4,493	20	1,472
7.	Prudential-Bache Securities	1,288.7	14,947	330	5,652
8.	Dean Witter Reynolds	1,213.6	17,801	656	7,543
9.	Bear, Stearns & Co.	1,057.2	5,472	12	1,879
10.	E. F. Hutton & Co.	986.4	18,051	450	6,680
11.	Morgan Stanley & Co.	901.2	4,212	6	1,311
12.	Donaldson, Lufkin & Jenrette	766.1	3,075	14	525
13.	Paine-Webber	635.1	12,833	284	4,444

14.	Kidder, Peabody & Co.	595.5	6,866	74	2,251
15.	Stephens	418.8	294	1	142

DUMONT BILLINGS:
THE BROKER AS ENTREPRENEUR

Dumont ("Dusty") Billings didn't start out to become a broker, let alone have her own brokerage firm. In fact, the road to selling tax-advantaged investments through Dumont Billings Ltd., was a rather winding one.

"I was a '60s kid in design school," she recalls. "I moved [from the East Coast] to New Mexico to study art. Going to the mountains was a big deal in the '60s. But you had to be, in my opinion, a little crazy to be an artist, and I was very interested in getting myself cooled out and straight. When I decided to drop out of art and go back to college, the University of New Mexico at Albuquerque was one of the top ten universities in experimental psychology. I graduated in experimental psychology with honors, moved to Boston and started doing research in psycholinguistics

*at MIT." It looked like the road was leading to a career in aca-
demia, but as Billings notes, "I'm a very outgoing person, and I
felt like parts of me weren't being used."*

*So Billings entered the master's program in clinical psychology
at Columbia University. She also got married. Not everyone
around her was convinced that psychology was what she should
be studying. "My father-in-law kept saying, 'You should be in
sales.'" Nevertheless, Billings went on for her master's, but again
her father-in-law kept saying, "Why are you dealing with people's
problems when you should be selling and being out there as a
go-getter." The truth was that Billings didn't actually enjoy her
work as a therapist. She started wondering, "What are people
doing to make money? Who are these people with briefcases walking down the street?"*

*She did some career research and realized that her forte was in
being with people. She was good at persuading and talking to
people. "I didn't want to sell cars or shoes. What did I want to sell?
My Dad's been big in the stock market for years. It just seemed
natural to show up selling stock, even though I didn't even know
what a bond was in those days. You can start with zip and become
a stockbroker."*

*Not having a background that would seemingly prepare her for
becoming a broker didn't intimidate Billings. She simply went to
the phone book and made a list of the major brokerage firms and
then got the names of all the branch managers. She interviewed
people she knew to make certain this was the kind of work she
wanted to do, put together a resumé and a cover letter, and then
walked into the branch managers' offices—cold, without an appointment, just like that. The result: "Many of them sat down and
interviewed me, because it's a very aggressive business. They liked
[the fact] that this person walked in with her briefcase and business suit. When I want something, I go get it, and I knew I wanted
this. You wouldn't do what I did if you wanted a job as a lawyer,
but they liked this girl with guts, because they figured, 'If she does
this with me, then she'll do the same thing to bring in the business.'"*

Still, with no solid background in sales, Billings found it difficult to get hired. That didn't stop her, though. When she met someone at Bache who was impressed with her but couldn't convince personnel to bring her in, Billings went back to the man and asked who else he knew and could he help her. He was so bowled over by her gutsy attitude that he sent her right over to Merrill Lynch where someone owed him a favor. "We had such an excellent interview. By this time I knew it was a sales position. I knew [the interviewer at Merrill Lynch] was going to say, 'Why should I hire you when you haven't had any sales experience?' And I had actually written out what to say after other interviews when it hadn't worked, and now I knew what to say." Suddenly Billings found herself with a job.

In 1980, she went through the training program, got her broker's license, and, she recalls, "got thrown out there with a telephone and a desk. 'Okay, bring in business,' they said. That's when most people don't know what being a stockbroker is. They think it's [just] knowing what stocks to pick. Well, it's knowing whom to talk to and when they're fooling you about how much money they have and how much they really want to invest. And when you're a woman, they think, 'Here's a cute chick. I'll give her some nonsense and maybe she'll go out with me.'"

Despite the pitfalls, Billings quickly became a "hot rookie." She explains her success this way: "Part of it was that the market was very depressed when I started, and the money market rates were very high, so I kept bringing in money." But this is a modest explanation. The fact is that Billings did something most new stockbrokers don't—she walked into buildings and literally knocked on doors. She went into stores and asked to speak to the owners. "I was very physical and aggressive in geting my body out there and walking the streets looking for business. That's how I met my best clients. One meeting like that is worth ten phone calls." From these initial clients came others through referrals. "As soon as you start making money for one person, they send all their friends."

Billings stayed at Merrill Lynch for two years as an account *executive before a headhunter (an executive recruitment company) found her a job at Smith Barney, where for the next year she was a senior account executive. "Brokers get prospected by headhunters all the time," Billings notes. "They say, 'Oh, we've heard you're doing really well. Can we place you?' Of course, they get a nice fee." Billings made the move to Smith Barney so that she could learn more about tax shelters, an area that firm was particularly strong in. She cut a deal where she was taken off commission and put on salary, and she started wooing important clients.*

This was great. But after a while, Billings said to herself, "Hey, what am I doing? I'm spending all this time making big ticket items, and I'm getting paid a third of that. Smith Barney's getting all of it." She met someone around this time who said, "You should start your own brokerage firm." Yeah, sure, was Billings' initial response. But the man kept pressing her. "All you have to do is pass the test [that will allow you to work as a principal and not just for an already existing firm]. Mr. Merrill did it. Mr. Smith did it. You're not any dumber than they were."

Billings decided that the man had a point. She took herself to Leo Fleur, a company that helps brokers pass their tests. She went every day to classes and after a few months took the exam that allowed her to work as a principal. Soon after, Dumont Billings Ltd., specializing in tax-advantaged investments, stock and bond funds, and personalized service, was born. "For two years I ran my own firm, alone," she recalls. "I had an accountant, of course, and occasional secretarial help, but I did everything. I knew I couldn't handle it myself anymore. I wasn't able to do the operations, the paperwork, deal with the NASD [National Association of Securities Dealers]—it was too much."

So Billings sold the company, which turned out to be a very smart move. Because she's been retained as the firm's only principal and also acts as a consultant, she still gets a percent of whatever they earn. "It's terrific to go to the beach while other people are earning money for you."

Now Billings and one of the buyers of her original company have started another corporation called Strategic Planning Group. They sell mutual funds and syndication deals in areas such as oil and gas and real estate. And, ironically, they plan to buy back into Billings' original company, which is in the process of being restructured.

Looking back on owning her own brokerage firm, Billings reflects, "I made a lot more money than I borrowed, which is fun, but it's much more of a lofty experience than most people realize to start your own company." As for the future, she doesn't plan on selling mutual funds for long. She and her partner are directing their energy toward real estate ventures allowing benefits for investors in the form of investment tax credits. "I'm not interested in selling mutual funds," she says, "It's too Mickey Mouse. I want to make $20,000 a shot. If you're going to spend an hour talking with a potential client, you might as well be making a potential $20,000 as $2,000. The sale is just as hard."

CHAPTER 5

TRADERS:
DEALING WITH
UNCERTAINTY

W hen you hear the words "Wall Street," what's the first
image that flashes on your mental screen? The floor of
the New York Stock Exchange, an aerial view showing a cha-
otic swarm of humanity rushing around under Big Brother-
style monitors. Turn on the sound, and the screaming you
hear doesn't help you make sense of the scene. "2 ½ for 200!"
"How are they?" "200 at 3!" "Take'm!" "Sold!" It's hard to
believe that there is a pattern to this dance and a translation to
the song, and even harder to believe that national economies
revolve around what takes place on the floors of the various
exchanges.

In New York the action runs from 9:30 A.M. when the
opening bell sounds to 4 P.M. when the bell peals the day's
close. And action is definitely the operative word. Traders
must have the fastest paced job on Wall Street. Fortunes can
be, and are, made and lost literally in seconds. The trading
day is six and one-half hours, five days a week of concentrated stress and strain and potential big gain. For those who
are temperamentally suited, it's a thrilling way to make a living.

WHO ARE THOSE GUYS AND
WHAT ARE THEY DOING?

There are so many men and women on the floor of the Exchange, gesturing, striding, screaming, phoning. Who are they and what are their jobs? Knowing a bit about who's who and what they do helps demystify the beehive of activity. Let's take a look at the New York Stock Exchange.

Stock market operations employees who work on the floor wear colored jackets to clarify their designations. They include:

Pages/Runners/Messengers/Squads. Wear light blue jackets. They run messages from the brokers to the booths.

Reporters. Wear navy blue jackets. They record all sales and changes of quotations and sizes for the stocks assigned to them. This information ends up on the ticker tape and other electronic information systems.

Supervisors. Wear green jackets. Each is in charge of a post, and they supervise their employees at that post.

Then there are managers, directors, assistant vice presidents, vice presidents, and executive vice presidents, all wearing street clothes, not jackets. They work "upstairs" and may not spend a lot of time on the floor itself, but they do come and go.

In addition to these stock exchange employees, there are the employees of the member firms. The Exchange Constitution permits a maximum of 1,366 members. When you first see the trading floor, you might assume all brokers are the same, but they aren't. There are five categories of market professionals active on the trading floor:

Commission Brokers work for member firms. They buy and sell for the firm's customers.

Independent Floor Brokers are individual entrepreneurs who act for a variety of clients.

Registered Competitive Market Makers have specific obligations to trade for their own or their firm's accounts—when called upon by an Exchange official—by making a bid or offer that will narrow the existing quote spread or improve the depth of an existing quote.

Competitive Traders, also known as dealers, trade for their own accounts.

Stock Specialists are the auctioneers in the Exchange marketplace. Specific stocks are assigned to them, and they are the focus of the market for those stocks. They work from their trading post on the floor. A broker who is interested in trading a particular stock will approach the specialist and ask, "How's XYZ Corp.?" The specialist brings buyers and sellers together. Specialists also risk their capital to ensure the maintenance of liquidity in a fair, orderly, and competitive exchange market for listed stocks. So specialists wear four hats: auctioneer, agent, dealer, and market catalyst.

WHAT'S GOING ON

Companies such as AT&T, IBM, Xerox, and Sony are listed on the New York Stock Exchange. Financial institutions such as Salomon Brothers and PaineWebber are members of the Exchange. The companies offer shares of their stock, which the financial institutions and investors buy and sell for their own and their clients' accounts. This is the simplest explanation possible, and of course the permutations are not nearly as straightforward. Still, this is the basic idea.

THE FAMOUS TICKER TAPE

You've heard of ticker tape, if only in connection with parades. Those strips of paper, which print out a constantly running update of stock information used to be read and then tossed down to the street from high-up office windows during parades. These days, since the tape runs via screens and monitors and not onto strips of paper, ticker tape is only pulled out for festive occasions. If you flip on your TV to one of the cable stations like Financial News Network (FNN), you'll see the tape running along the bottom of the screen. Here's how to read it:

Each stock is identified by a one-, two-, or three-letter code. For example, Ford is F, Eastman Kodak is EK, and IBM is IBM. Just below and to the right of the ticker symbol is the number of shares traded and the price. So F (Ford) may be trading at 58 ½ (100 shares were traded at $58.50 a share). When a sale of more than 100 shares is made, the zeros are dropped and the first digit (or digits) is printed before the price. 2s49 ½ would mean 200 shares traded at $49.50 a share. 12s68 ½ would mean 1200 shares traded at $68.50 a share. A double s indicates a ten-share unit stock, as opposed to 100 or above. It looks like this: 10ss. Other codes give additional information about a stock, such as "pfa" which means Preferred Series A. This would appear after the name of the stock.

THE WORLD OF THE TRADER

You may be surprised to learn that not all trading is done on the floors of the exchanges. Far from it. Large firms and smaller firms have their own trading desks where such business is often conducted. This is what they look like: a large room with lots of desks jammed against each other, computers and monitors stacked up everywhere, cigarette haze and desks littered with coffee cups and lunch remains. Traders, most of them young, stand or sit at the desks, phones at their ears, eyes on the screens, loudly talking the language of trading, quite possibly yelling it. Thanks to the wonders of modern technology, traders can work from almost anywhere. All you need is the hookup.

Essentially, a trader buys or sells securities—bonds, stocks, commercial paper, certificates of deposit, treasury bills—either for clients, from whom they collect a fee, or for their own firm. Sylvia Rocco, vice president of the Securities Trading Division at Merrill Lynch, is an extremely successful trader of listed equity stocks. She gives this example of a typical transaction:

"A customer calls into Merrill Lynch, say it's Dupont Pension, and says, 'Sylvia, we want to buy 100,000 shares of IBM.' (I'd love to actually get an order like that! I'm getting commissioned on that order.) What we try to do is find the other side of the trade, find the seller that may be out there. You have a hundred other people just like me at Merrill calling accounts all over the country saying we are a buyer of 100,000 IBM. Maybe we find a seller at 50,000. We've got half the trade done. If the customer has asked or if it fits for us, we may then put up our own money and fill in with the other 50,000. So what we have are people like me closing the accounts. Then we have people who are actively trading Merrill Lynch's own capital, making the decision, 'Should we short this 50,000 IBM or should we not short it?' "

Transactions like that one occur at a fast and furious pace, and of course scads of them are taking place at the same time. And it's not only stocks that are being traded. Trading has expanded to include just about anything you can think of and then some. All kinds of commodities, from pork bellies to cocoa to freight, are traded. Creative financial whizzes continue to come up with new instruments to trade, some so abstract that they literally do not exist. You can, for instance, trade futures contracts. But more about that in the next chapter.

Arbitrage, a word we've all heard a lot recently, is a type of trading. Arbitrage strategy involves simultaneously buying a contract in one market (e.g., gold in New York) and selling in another market (e.g., gold in London). The selling price is higher than the buying price, and in this way profit is locked in because of the momentary price difference. Arbitrageurs capitalize on risk created by uncertainty.

When we think of arbitrage, it's usually in relation to one company being taken over by another. This is the tie-in between mergers and acquisitions and arbitrage that we read about in the papers. In these cases, arbitrageurs buy and sell stocks based on the type of M & A deal that has been put together. Arbitrage has become quite glamorous these last few years, not to mention newsworthy. Ivan Boesky is perhaps the best-known arbitrageur. *Business Week* (August 13, 1984) described an arbitrageur this way: " . . . a trader who thrives on rumors, buying up shares quickly on hints of a raider's interest, in the hope of reselling them to anyone willing to pay a premium for control of a company."

Although trading has been around for a long time, only in recent years has it taken on a cache. One successful trader in his mid-thirties remembers how, when he was at Harvard Business School in the mid-1970s, trading was considered to be beneath MBA status. "Some of my classmates at Harvard," he recalls, "when I told them I was becoming a trader, thought, 'What happened? Did something go wrong?'" Hardly. Something went very right when this forward thinker decided early in his career that options were going to be an exploding market and settled on options arbitrage.

Options arbitrage developed from a very simple business of buying a put and selling a call on an individual stock. From there it has expanded into program trading, in which there are puts and calls on the entire stock market, instead of only on a single stock. It's precisely these kinds of immensely sophisticated and creative strategies that have created huge opportunities for traders.

Which brings us back around to the glamour image that trading has taken on of late. Here's what another veteran trader has to say on the subject. "I think [trading has developed a glamorous image] because it's a business where people can get ahead very quickly, where you hear stories all the time of people making a great deal of money at a very young age, where you can yell and scream and curse all day long and no one's going to say anything to you, where you can get out all your aggressions. If you work in a middle management position in some Fortune 500 company, you can't yell at people. That's just not part of the corporate culture. In the Wall Street trading community, that's what it's about. It has this very 'do what you want during the day' image, and that seems to be very appealing to people.

"I think what people don't understand, the nonglamorous aspect, is that you are a slave to your job all day long. You don't get to go out for a walk if you feel like it for fifteen minutes. The guy on the other side of you knows your personal business because you sit three feet away from him, and if you want to have a private conversation with someone, you can't. There are very few jobs where you wake up at 3:00 A.M. with a [ticker] tape dancing through your head. You live your job; you live your positions. The business becomes a part of you, and I don't know what you want to call that, but it's certainly not glamorous. Yes, it's a fun, exciting profession, but it's not for everyone. You've got to have the personality and ability to deal with the ups and downs of this business because there are a lot of them and they happen all the time."

Another trader adds: "It's a manic-depressive business, because you're either way up or way down. One minute things are great, and the next they're horrible. I also consider it to be an infantile business, because it gives you immediate gratification. You're like a junkie on a constant high, and you need your fix. When you're really trading and things are going well and it's busy and active, well, you're flying. You need to do more trading to keep that high going. Then when it slows down or starts to turn against you, it's as if you're crashing. That's not a pleasant feeling."

But that same trader is quick to add that he wouldn't be happy doing anything else. "It kind of ruins you for other work," he admits. "It's one of the few areas of business left today where you're your own boss, and once you've gotten into the habit of running the show, it's hard to work for another person."

Beyond these pros and cons there are other reasons for the appeal of trading. For one thing, since you can do business only during market hours (9:30 to 4:00 in New York, though obviously markets in other parts of the country and the world are on a different clock), your work day is set, and you have more free time than most other Wall Streeters. Analysts always seem to have a report to write, and investment bankers' duties often take them into the wee small hours. But with trading, your evenings and weekends are more your own. This means you never have to give away your theater tickets at the last minute because the meeting is running late or disappoint your children by missing the big baseball game because you suddenly have to go out of town.

On the other hand, the hours that the market is open are intense ones. At what other job is going to the bathroom a major decision? With trading, though, you wonder, "Am I going to miss a trade? Is something going to come across the tape? Is a big customer going to ring?" Although ostensibly traders make their own hours, the truth is that they never take time off. If things are slow you don't want to leave because the next trade could make your day; and if it's busy you don't want to walk away from the opportunities.

But traders don't seem to mind. They talk about how exciting it is to be in the center of the action, to get to react immediately to news events. The arbitrage trader quoted above has both Dow Jones and Reuters ticker tapes running in his office, and he is constantly checking them and making decisions based on the news they present. Adds another trader, who deals in commodities, "Commodity trading is the guts of the world economy in many ways because so many countries are dependent upon the revenues of their commodity exports."

Another thing that traders always mention when they talk about their job is the gratification of seeing instant results. As one trader puts it, "At the end of each day you see exactly how you've done. It's right there in living color. Either you made money or you lost money. And tomorrow you get to start fresh."

There's a fierce sense of competition, but also a feeling of team spirit. From one trader: "It's a game I like to win." "You want badly to get that trade done," says another. "But getting tough doesn't mean stomping the enemy. It's more about being able to capitalize on a situation, to seize the opportunity at precisely the optimum moment." His voice becomes almost rhapsodic. "One of the great things is the camaraderie on a trading desk. I don't think it's like anything else in any other business. You are with these people for such a long, concentrated stretch of time. It's so fast and so competitive that politics is really minimal during the day. Good friendships tend to develop, sometimes you know so much about the other person that there's nothing embarrassing."

INTERVIEW: WITH SYLVIA ROCCO
VICE PRESIDENT,
SECURITIES TRADING DIVISION
MERRILL LYNCH

As one of the first women traders, Sylvia Rocco gives a different perspective to the often macho world of trading. She also is one of the rare breed who, instead of jumping all over the Street, has stayed with the same firm for her entire career. For these two reasons, plus the fact that Rocco is a pro, her story and her views are worth hearing.

The summer after her second year in college Sylvia Rocco began working at Merrill Lynch, and "what started out to be a summer job turned out to be a permanent job because I met my future husband at Merrill Lynch. I was nineteen. We got married in 1971. I was working as an assistant to two institutional brokers at that time. They are both wonderful guys and still good friends. Their theory was that the more I did the more they could do with customers. So they just sort of shoved everything on me and said, 'Figure this out. Do this. Learn this.' It was a wonderful way of learning the business from the ground up. At that time there were very few women in trading. None at Merrill Lynch, and I would think if there was none at Merrill Lynch, there was none anyplace else either. Very few in research or investment banking or any of the other areas. No women in sales at all.

"Around this time, I think it was in the late '70s, the 'women's thing' came onto the floor, and Merrill Lynch was sued by some-one who applied for a job and didn't get it. So they said anyone who has been registered, which I was, and hasn't had a chance to go through the training program and become an account executive will have this chance. I grabbed it.

"When I came back [from the training program], I discovered that they didn't really want me to be an institutional broker. [I had been] sort of kidding myself, you know. Around this time the head of trading discovered that he had to have some women, too. All the traders knew me because I had worked pretty closely with them in my other job. They said, 'Well, okay, you're hired.' It was great. I remember getting a $5,000 raise, and it was just the best thing that ever happened. I went up to the trading room and started out covering things that nobody else wanted to do, retail, small orders, backup when somebody was out to lunch, and so on.

"As time went on I would sit with different traders on the desk as seating habits changed and pick up different things from trad-ers—different styles, ways of selling, points about the market. And I just sort of learned. Now I have about twenty-four accounts. Some are very large. I'm making an awful lot of money and am doing fine. [As for the macho side of trading,] I don't go out

drinking [with the other traders]. I don't go to hockey games [with clients]. It doesn't have to be done that way."

Q: What is your job called?

A: Coverage trader. Sales trader sometimes it's called. I don't trade capital for Merrill's account. What I do is call on the accounts, try to get the orders from them, and try to match them with the orders that we have on the desk.

Q: Trading gets very confusing to me. There seem to be so many kinds.

A: Just to make it simple, I work on the listed traded equity desk, so I'm trading listed stocks, nothing over the counter. That's a whole separate area. Now right next to us we have the arbitrage area.

Q: What happens there?

A: They may arb a common stock against a preferred stock. Or against a convertible bond. They may play these LBOs [leveraged buyouts,] and takeovers that you read about. They may say, 'Hey, we think that something may happen with this company. We want to be in on it.' So they'll buy some for Merrill Lynch and be involved in running those positions. We've got the options area, where traders do just what I do, except with options. And also trading Merrill's capital with options. This is interesting to watch because it all fits together. Sometimes one of my arbitrage guys may say, 'Hey, I want to be a buyer of XYZ because it's going to be taken over.' I keep track of all the holdings that my customers have, and I say, 'I know somebody who loans this.' So I call them and say, 'I have guys that want to buy this. What are your thoughts?' And they may say, 'Maybe up five points we'll sell it.' Or 'Why is your arb guy buying?' You get a conversation going, get the information going. You may get a trade out of it today or in a year or not at all, but it may help somebody else on the desk to generate orders. It's a real team effort. Sharing.

Q: How many people do you have in your area?
A: On the New York coverage desk we have about twenty people covering accounts. We have about fifteen position traders. Then we have the people that cover all the branch offices. So the whole kitandkaboodle may be about eighty people. That's just our area. The room is huge, and there are about 300 people in the room.

Q: Is the money you make based on a commission?
A: Yes.

Q: What is the commission usually?
A: It varies with the types of accounts you have and the firm you are with. I have twenty-four accounts, and each account is different. You can't really say it's a hard and fast 10 percent or 5 percent or 3 percent or 20 percent.

Q: It varies that much?
A: I'm sure. I don't know what the range is at other firms. You have to negotiate your own deal wherever you go. It's a lot lower on institutional business than it would be in retail.

Q: Because you're getting more volume?
A: Exactly. It's a whole different structure.

Q: How long does a client stay with you?
A: Years. I have accounts that have been with me for ten years.

Q: So it's really a long-term relationship.
A: It really is. That's what you have to worry about, rather than one trade. Trying to build something up. I tell customers a lot of times 'I don't think you should be doing this order with

me. I really think you should go across the street and talk to
somebody else, because they have a better handle on what's
going on in this stock.' Usually when you do that you get
three orders back. Because people appreciate that. I think
most people can tell if you're being honest and aboveboard
with them, and if they can trust you, that's what you want
them to do. It's a lot easier to get business done when you
know who you're talking to and what you're dealing with, and
not have to be afraid of someone.

Q: One of the main things I wanted to talk to you about is
the women's side. I've been getting the feeling that trading
is a real Boy's Club.
A: It is. You know you're working in a world where you are
outnumbered. And a lot of the talk is screaming and hollering
at someone, which you have to do about twenty times a day.

Q: Why are you screaming?
A: Well, if something isn't being done right. Maybe I
missed a trade. It could be any number of reasons. You may
not agree with the way someone is handling something for
you. And they don't agree with you, so it gets into something
more than just a friendly discussion.

Q: But it's absolutely acceptable behavior.
A: Oh, it's very much acceptable. Except a lot of times, if
you're a female, they say, 'You bitch,' which can be very
annoying. So it's a Boy's Club as far as that goes. But you just
have to learn to deal with it. And it's going to change because
more and more women are being hired.

WHAT MAKES A GOOD TRADER

"A trader is a trader is a trader," quoth one who knows. Ger-
trude Stein, who said much the same about a rose, would proba-

bly agree. Whether trading baseball cards or stocks or pork bellies, traders tend to share certain characteristics. Though it's not exactly fair to generalize, and certainly every generalization has its exceptions, most professionals will describe a particular kind of person who makes it in the rough-and-tumble world of trading. This head of trading sums it up well when he talks about what he looks for in an applicant:

"It doesn't matter whether you majored in economics or biology or music appreciation. The most important things are the ability to concentrate and the ability to answer a question asked during the interview decisively and quickly and to have confidence in your answer. This isn't a business where you have a lot of time to second guess yourself, and if you do, you're going to burn out immediately because we all make bad decisions when we trade. You can't look back; you've got to go on to the next trade.

"I like people who understand and are sophisticated about certain gambling events, be it horse racing or the tables. It's a concept of understanding odds, it's a concept of understanding risk, it's a concept of folding when you realize you've got a bad hand. You can go the other extreme, too. Bad gamblers and people who are addicted to gambling make bad traders. It's a riverboat mentality, and you don't want somebody like that." Tied into the gambler's mentality is a mind for math. Though you certainly don't need a Ph.D. in math, a natural ease with numbers helps. Not all good traders are gamblers in the most obvious sense. Some are attracted to games like chess or backgammon or Scrabble. Others like bridge. You probably can even find a trader or two who spends Wednesday nights at the church bingo game.

If the gambling analogy is a common one—and it is—so are comparisons between traders and athletes. A competitive spirit, mixed with loyalty to the team, is imperative for success. In both professions the physical and mental strain are terrific; tremendous concentration is required. For this reason and others, trading tends to be a game that men and women in their twenties and thirties play, and then quit. "It takes its toll," remarks one experienced trader. "After a while, people become more sales oriented or deal oriented. As you get older and your personal responsibilities increase—family, mortgage, all that—you tend to go toward a less risky line of work."

If burnout is a big factor for those who *can* handle the pressure, it's even more prevalent among people who don't belong in the business or who got in for the wrong reasons—like wanting to make a bundle of money but not having counted on the work being so hard. As that same trader puts it, "If you can't deal with the pressure cooker environment, you're going to get into a lot of trouble very quickly."

He cites this sobering statistic for his department: "Only one out of three people is here after the first year. It's an 'up or out' environment. It's also a very unstructured environment, because the ability to evaluate talent is absolutely clear-cut. You either make money trading or you don't. Bureaucracy is not needed, though strict discipline is." That same trader believes that traders get fired more quickly than many other professionals. "Sometimes you do it for the person's benefit, because you realize he is just not going to make it, and there's no sense carrying dead wood or leading someone astray."

Though this revolving door attitude doesn't say much for job security, what it does offer is plenty of opportunity for people to give trading a try. As in almost every corner of Wall Street, an MBA is desirable at many firms. Yet a surprising number report that they actually prefer recent college grads with no trading experience and no advanced degrees. Listen to what several heads of trading departments have to say:

"I don't expect anyone to have any idea what he's doing the first day he comes in here. It's on-the-job training. Seventy-five percent of the people we've hired have had no previous experience. We have chosen to take people from the undergraduate level. We want to train traders to trade the way we trade, and not to come in with any bad habits or be predisposed to trading with a different style."

"I'm not interested in MBAs. I want someone who is aggressive, has the ability to react under pressure, and has certain interpersonal skills. The last is important, because trading is really about dealing with other people. Despite the sophisticated communications equipment we have, the best trading is done with people you know and are close to and who know you. You can help people more if you understand what they are trying to do. So we mostly hire kids right out of college and work with them to develop relationships. The basic job is selling, and it doesn't matter sometimes how educated you are if you can't get people to trust you, and work with you, and open up to you."

"I'm looking for someone who has analytical skills, is good at relationship building, and (this is very important) is consistent and tenacious about watching for opportunities. In this business, everyone is sitting with his hand on the trigger. You can't blink or you lose."

"The pecking order [of a trading desk] naturally asserts itself when people work together so closely. If you show promise, you'll move up to a trading assistant or a clerical position. You can have a rather awesome amount of responsibility, albeit in a very narrowly defined way, in that you make decisions that are totally a matter of judgment and that earn or lose hundreds of thousands of dollars in a few seconds."

THE MONEY

You probably will start out with a relatively modest salary, in the low- to mid-20s, which actually is pretty fair considering that most traders are young and inexperienced.

From there, though, the progression is rapid. Merrill Lynch's Sylvia Rocco puts the average in the high six figures, though she has heard tell of one arbitrage trader who hit the million-dollar mark. But she also notes that "when business is bad, you die. It goes in spurts. You'll be doing great, but it doesn't always last. You may go through a really dry period, just saying, 'What am I doing wrong? My customers hate me. I shouldn't be in this business.' It can be troubling, it really can. You know you're not going to starve, but the money is sort of a measure of how well you are doing."

One trader puts it right on the line when he says, "Anyone who gets a position of responsibility and starts trading either from capital or on a very sophisticated basis should expect to make nothing less than six figures within the first two years. If you're not making that kind of money, either you're being grossly underpaid for what you're producing or you don't belong in trading."

CHAPTER 6

COMMODITIES TRADERS: UPPING THE STAKES

During the Renaissance, Venice waged salt wars to control the market. The powers to be were no fools. They knew that people could manage without traditional forms of currency, but not without salt. Some time later Napoleon Bonaparte noted that the futures of entire empires rested on sugar. Stocks and bonds and money in all their various forms are one thing, but commodities such as salt, sugar, grains, and metals are another. And not just in the world at large, but on Wall Street. Today trading these tangible items, as well as some intangible ones, is big business. It's called commodities trading. The global trade in basic food commodities alone totals more than $60 billion a year. After all, we all need food, so the market is assured.

Even though the worth of commodities has long been recognized, from Wall Street's vantage point, commodities came into their own around the 1969–1970 recession when the market was doing none too well. Despite the fact that commodities are extremely volatile, they had certain appeal. There was less paperwork and more turnover, so you could do business at a fast pace and, of course, realize greater profits. As attention turned to the world market, commodities soared to new heights and truly became Big Business. Commodities trading first got organized, though, on the first Monday of April 1848, when eighty-two businessmen formed the Chicago Board of Trade. Today, the seat of commodities trading is still Chicago, though New York holds its own, with some activity in Kansas City, Missouri, and Minneapolis. The major exchanges are as follows:

NEW YORK
Amex Commodity Exchange
Commodity Exchange Inc. (Comex)
New York Coffee, Sugar, and Cocoa Exchange
New York Cotton Exchange
New York Mercantile Exchange
New York Futures Exchange

CHICAGO
Chicago Board of Trade
Chicago Mercantile Exchange
International Monetary Market
Chicago Rice and Cotton Exchange
MidAmerica Commodity Exchange

KANSAS CITY, MISSOURI
Kansas City Board of Trade

MINNEAPOLIS
Minneapolis Grain Exchange

Trading is also done over the counter, that is, independently rather than through one of the exchanges.

Perhaps the most fascinating aspect of trading commodities is its integral relationship with natural disasters and world events. News breaks of an earthquake in Colombia, and quickly, the traders move coffee beans. A drought hits the Midwest and corn prices soar. Or better yet, something like the "great grain robbery" occurs. That happened in 1972 when the U.S. practically gave away its wheat crop to the Soviet Union, an act that depleted U.S. grain reserves and sent prices through the roof. Whatever their political opinions on the matter, from a business standpoint, commodities traders could not help but be delighted. In the world of commodities, one person's disaster is another person's good fortune (and that person is probably a trader). How's this for a not atypical news item: "Platinum prices posted strong, fresh increases yesterday, as traders bid up prices in response to unrest in South Africa, where much of the precious metal is mined."

A president of trading at one of the major firms was willing to speak candidly about the commodities business, but insisted that he not be identified. His clients, he said, count on his discretion, and his effectiveness depends on his relationship with his clients. Let's call this mystery trader Mr. X and his company, The Firm.

According to Mr. X, commodities and currencies, once a specialized merchant business, are now "one more row of items in the financial supermarket." On his floor of The Firm, metals, foreign currencies, and crude oil products are traded. There are additional offices in London and Singapore so that the world can be covered from a twenty-four-hour perspective, which is a good thing because the numbers Mr. X cites are staggering. Among their three market centers, $2 billion and $3 billion are traded daily. Not only that, but The Firm itself can own a billion dollars' worth of commodities at any one time. Despite this, Mr. X makes the very complex activities of his department sound as easy as a day at the beach.

"We buy and sell and transport and finance and process (except in the case of currencies, which you don't process) commodities in different forms, and deal with institutional customers, such as foreign governments and central banks, industrial consumers, mining companies, oil-producing companies, fabricators of electronics parts that use metals, jewelry companies, photographic companies, and chemical companies. We're dealers, not brokers. We don't tell people the future,

what the price will or won't be. We don't handle retail speculative business for private customers. We deal with institutional
customers, and what we provide is liquidity and service. We're
the center of the market. We're where people come when they
want to transfer their risk positions. They give them to us. You
know a mine is producing. They want a program to hedge and
transport and finance and process. We put together deals for
them. We do minute-to-minute trading. People call us for bids
and offers and virtually anything related to our markets. What
we try to do is get all the buyers and sellers in the world to come
to us, and then we take positions on for ourselves and try to
liquidate. These are current and future positions. They are not
positions on futures markets. They're forward positions. A forward position is a transaction in the future that does principal
between two parties. A futures transaction is done on the futures markets themselves via a broker. We're principals, not
brokers. [The same thing we do] is going on elsewhere in The
Firm in so-called soft commodities—cocoa, coffee, sugar, and
grain."

To further clarify how these transactions take place, Mr. X
continues: "What we try to do is liquify commodity positions for
people and make it as much like money as we can. Somebody
has something that may be a pile of dreck halfway on the other
side of the world, and he wants to get money quickly. We make
some part of that value for adding value to the transaction in
terms of getting him money sooner or getting him more money
than he could get for himself because we have more outlets for
the material."

"We may buy concentrates, which are a semi-mined form of
metal, and sell futures contracts, and lock in interest rates, and
charter a vessel, and book refining space, and apply the appro-
priate insurance, and put together the package. But we look at
everything. We don't take other than intraday price risk on the
commodity itself. We take a lot of what's called arbitrage risk
or differential risk or location risk or time-spread risk. We take
commercial risks, rather than market risks.

"Our market risks are limited to intraday because if a counter-party comes up and says, 'I'll sell you five tons of gold,' we're not going to be able to sell five tons of gold in two seconds. He may want to sell five tons of gold in two seconds, which is where we come in. We'll buy it, and then he doesn't have to call forty people and show his hand to the whole world. So we're constantly buying and selling all day. We also function as a 'beard' for those in the market whose activities may be defined as sensitive, particularly a foreign government that controls a major part of the world's production and doesn't want the rest of the world to know what it's doing."

One of the most fascinating aspects of Mr. X's work (and one that is not often mentioned in relation to Wall Street) is that he has the chance to be exposed to many different ideologies. As he puts it, "You deal with a lot of socialist countries and Third World countries, and you see production at its most elemental level—taking things out of the ground and adding value to them, first through a series of industrial processes and then financial processes."

TIME OUT TO DEFINE A FEW KEY WORDS

The following are key terms you'll hear often and want to understand:

Contract. A specified amount of a commodities contract to be delivered or received at a specified date and place for a specified price. Example: 25,000 British pounds for August 15 delivery at Barclay's Bank. (This example is for a futures contract. If it's an options contract, the owner has the right to act on the contract *up to* August 15.)

Call Option. The right to buy 100 shares of a particular stock or stock index at a fixed price before a preset deadline, in exchange for a premium. The deadline is usually three, six, or nine months. The call option buyer anticipates that the price will rise between the time he buys and the deadline.

Put Option. The opposite of a call option. Substitute "sell" for "buy." The thinking here is that the price is going to fall, not rise.

Position. How much of a security or market an investor holds.

Long Position. The number of shares *owned.*

Short Position. The number of shares *owed.*

Selling Long. Disposing of a contract.

Selling Short. Disposing of a contract not owned by the seller, in anticipation of a price drop and profiting from that drop.

Strike Price. The set price at which an option, during the time it is operating as an option, can be bought or sold.

Premium. The price a put or call buyer pays a seller.

Margin. The amount an investor puts up for a contract. It is much less than the actual value of the contract.

Leverage. The amount the bank or other investor puts up for a contract. (The margin and the leverage make up the whole price of the contract.) Leverage allows you to buy more of a certain entity than you could with just the money you have on hand. Example: A commodity is trading at 50. You have $5,000, and so you can buy 100 shares. But if you buy on margin, you may only have to put up 10 percent of your own money, so for $5,000 you can buy 1,000 shares. The other 90 percent, which is the leverage, is put up by a bank or other investor. Your leverage is 10 to 1. In a way, you've borrowed from Peter to pay Paul. If your stock makes money, you'll win big. But if your stock loses, you'll owe a lot of money.

FUTURES AND OPTIONS

As with commodities, Chicago is the place to be for futures and options. But Philadelphia, San Francisco, and New York also have active exchanges.

In the go-go world of Wall Street, options is the old lady on the block, having been important for all of about twenty years. Trading in options on futures, legally revived only since October 1982, is the new whiz kid.

We've all heard of a producer or an actor buying an option on a screenplay. That means the person has bought the right to make a movie from the screenplay by a certain date. If the movie doesn't get made, the option has to be renewed or the rights once again go on the open market. Either way, the screenwriter keeps the money that was paid for the option. Commodities options operate similarly. You choose whether or not to exercise your option by a predetermined date. If you think the value of the option will sink lower than the price at which you bought, you sell a put option. If you gamble that it will rise, you buy a call option.

Just what are you trading here? Commodities, though what that means precisely has changed. In 1974, the Commodity Futures Trading Act passed by Congress redefined commodities as anything "that is or becomes the subject of futures trading, intangible as well as tangible." That broadened the scope, to say the least. These days it's not just pork bellies and soy beans, but treasury bonds and money market futures. Ocean freight is a hot item. You're betting literally that your ship will come in and not get batted around the bend by a hurricane. Trading on stock indexes is another popular arena. Here you're gambling on which way the stock market will move via indexes, such as the Standard & Poor's 500 (a.k.a. S&P 500), which measures stock market changes based on how 500 common stocks perform. Notice the future tense—whether your ship will come in; which way the stock market will move. And in the case of the stock indexes, you're not even trading anything that really exists. Instead, your contract is for the imaginary delivery of an imaginary portfolio with a theoretical value . . . that nevertheless moves up or down and makes or loses investors' money.

With a futures contract, you agree to either buy or sell a specific amount at a set price by a predetermined date. Your task is to figure out whether the price will go up or down by that future date and then set your deal accordingly. A futures contract can sometimes be viewed as a kind of insurance policy. For instance, a farmer needs money to grow his crop. He contracts through a broker to sell the crop for a certain price when it's ready to harvest. Now the farmer can get loans from banks by using the contract as collateral. If the market value of his crop goes up, the farmer has lost out on that extra income, but if the price drops, he's done well for himself. Now, let's say that the farmer is growing wheat and that the buyer of the farmer's contract is General Mills, who needs the wheat for its cereals. By locking in the price of the wheat, General Mills is assured of getting tomorrow's crop at today's prices. Both sides are taking a big chance, of course, but one that serves their purposes. These are the hedgers (as in "hedging your bets").

In contrast to the hedgers, most speculators who play the futures market don't know soy beans from a sow's ear and couldn't care less about the difference. Speculators are in this to make money and to make it fast. They don't have to worry about finding a herd of cattle grazing on their front lawn one fine day, because they close out their position long before the contract expires. All they ever have to think about is the difference between the price at which they bought and the price at which they sold. They've either made money or lost it.

One of the main attractions of futures is that the investor only has to put down a small percentage of the actual contract value. This is the margin, and usually it's five percent. So for very little cash you stand to make big bucks. But, as with all alluring deals, you also stand to lose. And lose. And lose. If you sell short and the price keeps going up, you can end up owing quite a lot of money.

It's the sheer uncertainty of the game, the undeniable fact that the future holds no guarantees, that gives this area of trading its win big–lose big nature. "Volatile" is the word most often attached to futures trading. "Grueling" is a word often used to describe the life of these traders. And it's phrases like "the wilds of the futures pits" that give you the flavor of the exchanges. The uncertainty is such that traders commonly resort to superstition, carrying lucky charms or devising small rituals, to see them through. Many consult psychics, and most respond overwhelmingly to rumor.

Despite the pressures, commodities trading is attracting more young people than ever. In 1976 the Chicago Board of Trade had 1,402 members. By the third quarter of 1987, the number of members and membership interest holders topped 3,475. In 1980, the Commodity Futures Trading Commission listed approximately 4,000 traders on all regulated exchanges. By 1986, there were 6,400.

THE CRUELTY OF THE PIT

Think big. Think positive. Never show any sign of weakness. Always go for the throat. Buy low. Sell high. Fear—that's the other guy's problem. Nothing you have ever experienced can prepare you for the unbridled carnage you are about to witness. The Super Bowl, the World Series . . . they don't know what pressure is. In this building, it's either kill or be killed. You make no friends in the Pits and you take no prisoners. One

minute you're up half a million in soy beans and the next,
boom, your kids don't go to college and they've repossessed your
Bentley. Are you with me?

                       —from *Trading Places*

To call a membership in one of the exchanges "a seat" is great
irony, since there is no place on earth more hectic and certainly
no one sits down. Though each of the exchanges has its own
personality, what they all have in common is a frenzy that starts
when the opening bell shrills and doesn't let up for a single
instant until the closing bell chimes.

It's an exclusive club, and not a cheap one to join. For one
thing, there are a fixed number of seats. Seat prices depend on
supply and demand, the demand increasing whenever the market peps up. What a membership gives you is the right to trade
without going through a broker and paying high commissions.
For this privilege you pay several hundred thousand dollars, a
lot of beans to trade by anybody's standards. It is possible,
though, on many of the exchanges, to purchase a limited membership or to lease a seat for considerably less money. A limited
membership will allow you to trade a few specific contracts,
while a leased seat is a kind of rental arrangement. As for the
price difference, it's considerable. In early 1986, a seat on the
Chicago Board of Trade went for about $220,000; its limited
memberships ranged from $12,000 to $68,000.

What you get for your money is admittance to what might be
described as a legalized loony bin. Traders as finely pitched as
thoroughbreds stand around in the morning thinking and talking
about little other than what the market did yesterday and what
it will do today. There's a camaraderie and a loyalty to be sure,
but bang, once that opening bell peals, all hell breaks loose. It's
every man for himself, because one person's loss is another's
gain. A Philadelphia trader sets the mood: "Your competitor is
standing right next to you. They're your friend . . . but they're
not. Theoretically, if they make money, it's money you didn't

make. Trading is as much understanding human psychology when you're in the crowd as anything else. It's like being in a poker game. You have to be able to read someone's face, to see how they're taking the pressure. You have to know how to stroke people. There's all sorts of gamesmanship."

A Chicago trader put it this way: "I don't care if you're from Yale or Yonkers. I don't care if you were a straight-A student or never got past the ninth grade. Here in the Pit we're all the same." Another trader adds: "This never used to be a job for the educated gentleman. It was more for smart-ass kids short on lineage but long on chutzpah. But it's changed. Today everyone wants to get in on the game. The Pit has become the chic place to see and be seen. But you know what, where you're from doesn't change a thing. You strike or get struck out."

Sometimes the striking gets literal. It's likely that many more men than women enter the Pit because it's not only emotionally rough but physically rough. Commodities traders are well known for their single-minded devotion to making the trade. There's no time for gentle manners. If the Pit is a gritty scene of screaming and gesturing and pushing, so raucous that veterans commonly report such ailments as permanently pinched nerves, throat disorders, high blood pressure, and even broken bones, it's also a scene that has its attractions.

Unlike most jobs, the Pit holds office politics at bay. Combat is direct but without malice; you know just where you stand, both with your colleagues and with your accounts. At the end of each day you tally up your score, and the next morning you start fresh. With your order cards clutched in your hand and your feet planted to the spot you've claimed like the head of a street gang protecting his turf, you know exactly where you are and why. The uncertainty doesn't lie there, but in what will happen on the board and how well you'll handle it. For many, that's the daily challenge, and the rush. It's also an independent type of work, best suited to those who prefer autonomy. It's common to hear commodities traders talk about how they could never work in a "regular office." Finally, though, the greatest attraction to jumping into the Pit is the possibility of making a lot of money fast. No matter what other qualities a trader has, there's not one who doesn't have at least a touch of the dreamer about him. Says one, "You go in there every morning with your heart racing. Today could be the day."

GETTING STARTED

Commodities traders cut their teeth in the Pit by working as runners and clerks. The money at this stage isn't exactly stunning—about $100 to $150 a week for runners and $15,000 to $35,000 a year for clerks. After you've done your duty, the next step is to buy or lease a seat. In addition to the not inconsiderable amount of money you need for that (which was discussed a few paragraphs back), you'd best have at least $25,000 to work with if you'll be trading for your own account. Naturally, you don't need that start-up money if you go to work for a firm, which might also help bankroll your seat.

A Philadelphia trader with his own firm (you'll meet him in a minute) explains how bankrolling works: "We set guys up to trade. They don't need a lot of capital to go into business. We provide the capital, we train them with our own training tapes and send them through a course. We let them go out there and trade, and then they're in business. They can make real dollars, more money than they could make anywhere else.

"Trading for yourself is the greatest. You have your own business. You have your clearing agent. Individuals don't clear trades themselves, they use a clearing agent, who charges so much per contract and acts as your bank. They provide capital, margin money. The clearing agent also takes care of your bookkeeping and provides you with an office, a secretary, and medical benefits. It's great. But the downside is that you become a general creditor of the clearing agent, so that if someone else who is trading takes down the clearing agent, they could take you down with them. You just have to choose carefully, that's all."

Once you actually begin trading, what you make depends entirely on your skills and whatever other forces rule the Pit. Most likely, you'll end up being what's known as a scalper—a trader who goes for volume, figuring that if you make enough trades you've got to come out all right in the end. The majority of scalpers specialize in one commodity, buying and selling hundreds of contracts a day, flipping them quickly, often within seconds or fractions of a second, and earning small amounts, maybe only $15, with each trade. Those pennies can add up to a six-figure income. Still, it's not an easy way to earn a living.

This is definitely a sweaty palms profession. Traders live with fear in their gut, but the mark of a true professional is how he plays the game when his position is going against him, as it all too frequently does. Everyone has bad days where he loses his shirt and maybe his pants, too. It's the traders who can ride through those periods that make it for the duration. All others are out the door and knocking on another. If you ask a trader what he thinks is the single-most important quality for success, he'll likely tell you it's discipline—the discipline to control feelings of fear and greed, to trade within your limits, to hold your profits and close out your losses, to trust your instincts and your judgment, and to ride out the bad times. One trader provided the following prescription: "Trading is 98 percent emotional and 2 percent intellectual."

THE VIEW FROM PHILADELPHIA

Many traders are admittedly superstitious. Like the gamblers and athletes to whom they're so often compared, they fear "losing the touch," and do whatever they can to guard against this. Allowing themselves to be identified in print is one of the things some traders seem to think might jeopardize their success, and it is, frankly, why of all the traders quoted in these two chapters, only one—Sylvia Rocco—would speak on record. One Philadelphia options trader (we'll call him Mr. Trader) summed up the general mood: "Go ahead, use whatever I say, only please don't mention my name. If you do, I'll worry all night. I won't be able to sleep. And if things don't go well tomorrow, I'll just know it's because of this conversation."

Articulate and successful, Mr. Trader is an excellent example of today's options trader. That's why we'll let him speak from behind his screen.

A thin, energetic man in his late thirties, Mr. Trader trades for himself through several firms. One is entirely his own; the other is a joint trading agreement he has with two other men. Within this partnership, they have other people who trade for them. Mr. Trader himself spends every day in the center of the action, right on the floor of the Philadelphia exchange trading stock options.

When asked how he got involved in the business, he says, "My family was into it. After I graduated from Temple University with a degree in finance and insurance, I was planning to go to Wharton [School of Finance of the University of Pennsylvania]. But I had a great-uncle whose firm was a member of the New York Stock Exchange. He was getting up in years, and I didn't know how much longer he'd be in the business. I wanted to get some experience in with him. I did everything you can do. I was a runner on the street, I did back office work, computer work. I traded equities, did block trading, institutional trading.

"After a half dozen years or so, I found that I was bored. I was going to move into reinsurance and insurance brokerage, but listed options had just started in Chicago. I thought it looked like a pretty good game. So I went out to the CBOE [Chicago Board Options Exchange] and then came back to Philadelphia when the Exchange opened here."

Having seen the business from the three main cities from

which it is conducted, Mr. Trader has interesting observations about the differences between them: "There are different styles of trading in Chicago, New York, and Philadelphia. The fellows in Chicago originally came out of the commodities end of the business, so they are hedge-oriented. The fellows originally on the Amex [Commodity Exchange] came from stock trading, equity trading, and they basically had what we would call a Delta position background. That means they are share-equivalent position-oriented. It's more of a non-hedge trading position. So they want it to be just long or short. You know, they like the stock (when I say stock, the options are in the stock, so it's important that you either like the stock or you don't). In Philadelphia, I'd say we had a combination of both.

"Because this Exchange opened later than the others, we didn't have the IBMs, the Union Carbides, the General Motors, the Eastman Kodaks—the Dow stocks. We had options on the secondary companies. In some ways, this turned out to be good for us. Nobody was going to take over IBM, but we probably had more takeovers on our Exchange proportionally than on any other Exchange. This made for a different trading style—one where we traded a lot of stock against our positions—because our issues were more volatile, and the liquidity wasn't as good since these weren't the high-capitalization stocks."

As for working on a smaller Exchange, it doesn't bother Mr. Trader. He points out that the options they trade are "primary markets" in Philadelphia, meaning they are not traded elsewhere. "For the options we trade," he says, "we *are* the market. Plus I know a lot of people in New York. I speak to all the traders. And I think we have as talented a group here as anywhere. Actually, we have some people here who also trade on the Amex. They count individually for the largest share of business done on the Amex. We feel pretty sure that if we can do that from down here in Philadelphia, we wouldn't have too much trouble doing it in New York."

PROFILE: RICHARD DENNIS,
COMMODITIES TRADER

In every profession there's one person who defies tradition, breaks all the rules, and comes out way on top. In commodities trading, that person is Richard Dennis. The world of money and markets captured Dennis at an age when most kids can't see past next week's allowance. He was only a teenager when he convinced his father to cough up $1,400 to purchase a trading badge at the small MidAmerica Commodity Exchange. Because he was underage (you had to be twenty-one), he also convinced his father, a school clerk with conservative investment standards, to stand in while Dennis directed from the sidelines. Starting with $400 lent by his brother, who earned it delivering pizzas, Dennis made his first million at twenty-five. The New York Times Magazine labeled him "Prince of the Pits" the year after that. Today, at thirty-eight, Richard Dennis is still on top.

What separates Dennis from the pack is his original and independent philosophy of trading. Early on he decided that he would go against the prevailing trading rule of "sleeping light." Translation: getting rid of your speculative positions before the closing bell each day. Instead, Dennis set up a system whereby he always held positions overnight, and by going against the traffic, he made out very well. He also, over time, organized what he called "ideas," a list of technical information about the market and its movement, that became complex enough to feed into a computer. That, too, proved useful. Dennis's estimated personal worth hovers around $135 million.

In a world where emotions tend to rule, he's fully wedded to the concept of strategies. "The people who are winning [at commodities]," he told Forbes (October 27, 1986), "are following successful strategies." The losers, he contends, call the commodities game a big casino, whereas the winners think of it as a fine institution where economic necessity meets speculative ability. He believes in "being persistent, consistent, and intense."

Dennis thinks big. In addition to trading about $100 million of his own capital, he has a management firm, Richard J. Dennis & Co., in Chicago, that manages futures funds and accounts (minimum investment: $500,000) for individuals. He'll often trade the limit, though because he's got so much to play with, that's only a small percentage of his capital. While we're talking percentages, it may be worthwhile to note that even brilliant Richard Dennis sees profits from only 5 percent of his trades. The rest are either losses or only marginally profitable. That's a sobering comment on the nature of commodities trading.

What also sets Richard Dennis apart is his personal style. For years, despite his great wealth, he lived an exceedingly low-key life. A heavyset man with dimples and thinning hair, he continued to live with his parents on the South Side of Chicago, and even today shares a place on Lake Shore Drive with his dad. (His mother passed away several years ago.) He was known for his rumpled polyester suits, obsession with baseball, and attraction to bar-and-grill type restaurants. Mostly, he was content to stare at his monitors. In more recent years, he's emerged a bit, and has even been seen at a White House dinner or two. He has developed a decided interest in politics and founded a liberal think tank, the Roosevelt Center for American Policy Studies. A second career in some aspect of politics seems not out of the question.

Richard Dennis maintains that successful commodities traders are not born, but taught. As if to prove his point, he took on the task of training a group of young traders a couple of years ago. He took out an ad in the Wall Street Journal, *culled a class from the 1,000 applicants, and introduced them to his contrarian methods. And how did these bright young risk-takers fare? Their success rate, Dennis claims, has averaged over 100 percent a year since he let them loose.*

CHAPTER 7

INTERNATIONAL BANKERS: DOLLARS TO POUNDS TO YEN

"The brave new world of global finance is here," stated reporters Michael R. Sesit, Ann Monroe, and Peter Truell in a special report on global finance and investing in the *Wall Street Journal* (September 29, 1986).

In myriad ways and with dazzling speed, hundreds of billions of dollars pour into one account and out of another around the world, around the clock: General Motors Corp. packages car loans as securities and sells them in Europe and Japan. British Telecommunications PLC offers stock in New York and Tokyo. The Industrial Bank of Japan issues sterling bonds in London. Deutsche Bank Capital Corp. arranges for a U.S. company to issue Euromark bonds and swap the proceeds into dollars with American, Japanese, West German and French banks and companies. The upending flow of money greases the machinery of the international financial markets as never before. It enables borrowers to find funds and lenders to seek the best return for their assets.

This, in a nutshell, is where the whirlwind world of international banking is positioned these days. Thanks in large part to the technology that has put the world at our fingertips, but also to the creativity of movers and shakers who keep coming up with new and different ways to package financial instruments, the international scene is at an all-time frenzy.

Many of the advancements in international banking can be traced back to the 1929 stock market crash and the depression that followed. It was then that banking was divided into strictly defined categories. The Glass–Steagall Act of 1933 in particular split the lending function and the investment function. Commercial banks got hold of lending, while investment banks took on underwriting and distribution of securities. Like a sister who marries well, the investment banks over the years have found themselves in a position to see large profits, while commercial banks have usually had to settle for more modest sums.

Even with deregulation blurring the lines of who does what, banking is not nearly as freewheeling in the U.S. as it is throughout the rest of the world where no such rules and regulations exist (with the exception of Japan, which has its own version of the Glass–Steagall law). Meanwhile, commercial banks are trying to get Glass–Steagall repealed, but so far, the law holds firm. It's with true American pioneering spirit, then, that U.S. commercial banks have seized the opportunity to do elsewhere what they're not allowed to do at home. With great zeal they have pushed off from the homefront to flex investment banking muscle on an international scale.

Lending to foreign governments and companies has always been a major part of international banking, and it remains key when discussing this area of the financial marketplace. But the big news is that commercial banks are expanding their horizons by adding securities to their activities. Much like investment banks in this country, they are creating exotic financial instruments—futures, options, swaps, ceilings, indemnities, option bonds, and the like—to lure investors.

Citicorp, J. P. Morgan & Co., and Bankers Trust are the top three U.S. commercial banks giving investment houses a run for the money of foreign clients. Not far behind them are Chase Manhattan, Chemical Bank, Manufacturers Hanover, and Security Pacific, among others, which have been beefing up investment banking operations since 1983.

The U.S. isn't the only nation to recognize that international securities is a race worth running. When London's Big Bang exploded in October 1986 (see later in this chapter for more on that event), England entered international markets with a rousing noise. Japan has been the leader of the pack, outracing even the U.S. during times when the dollar is weak. (More on Japan's role later in this chapter.) The Japanese have a tremendous amount of capital, more, even, when their currency is strong than the Saudi sheiks controlled a few years ago. Unlike the Arabs, who preferred stashing their surplus in bank accounts, the Japanese are keen on securities. This is one good reason why investments is the new centerpiece of international banking, and why U.S. bankers have a yen to see their dollars hit that market. As Thomas C. Theobold, former vice chairman of Citicorp and head of the Investment Bank sector and now chairman of Continental Illinois Bank in Chicago, told *Forbes* (July 14, 1986), "We are a broker/dealer/underwriter/distributor on every major and minor stock exchange in the world with one exception—the U.S."

HOW THE U.S. GOT INTO BANKING ABROAD

U.S. banks opened their doors to their foreign neighbors in the early 1970s. Citicorp, for example, had a string of storefront "money shops" in Britain. As one analyst remembers, however, "Nobody came in." Part of the problem, according to some experts, was that people tended not to trust their hard-earned cash to foreigners. Plus U.S. banks often did not fully understand the needs of a country's customers. Nor did they always understand the different laws, regulations, and restrictions. Consumer banking, as banking for little guys like you and me is called, did not translate from one country to another with any degree of success.

Yet, as one international banker explains it, "In the early 1970s, what banks were basically focusing on was simply to become a presence and to handle international financial transactions, primarily for subsidiaries of U.S. corporations. It was local borrowing, local letters of credit, and financial instruments in those countries for people you were already doing business with. In some countries, the U.S. came to dominate the marketplace, in Brazil, for example, where Citibank became the second leading bank. They expanded rapidly to handle Brazilian companies and local transactions. That spread to cross-border transactions when countries began to look for financing beyond one-on-one. They started to look to the bank in New York to syndicate in other countries. Suddenly, banks from all over the world were participating."

Even while banks were getting together in this new global way, a few institutions, notably Citicorp and Chase Manhattan, continued to concentrate as well on developing decently sized consumer banking departments in foreign countries. Having started in the 1970s in ten countries, Citicorp currently has stretched its reach to thirty-four countries. Most recently, it has bought retail banks in Belgium and Italy, broken into the mutual fund business in Brazil, and moved into mortgage financing and insurance in West Germany. Meanwhile, Chase has been one of the few American banks to scurry Down Under; in collaboration with an Australian insurance company it has established a commercial bank. BankAmerica, on the other hand, has dropped its plans to get into consumer banking in Australia and is generally pulling back from its forays into the foreign consumer marketplace.

Credit cards, of course, remain an active aspect of foreign banking. Not only American Express, but also the various banks that handle Visa and Mastercard have brought the world a little closer to home through those plastic cards that buy people almost anything they want.

An international banker at Bankers Trust sums it up: "In the last five years, the financial market has become one integrated global market. Today, if a company wants financing—say, an airline wants to finance the purchase of an aircraft—you break out the elements of the financing that company is looking for and you try to find the pocket in the world that's the most efficient at obtaining that element."

SOME TERMS YOU'LL WANT TO KNOW

Eurobonds. Traded mostly from London, Eurobonds are a major way that governments and huge corporations raise capital. The bonds may be issued in dollars or another currency. The underwriting group is usually comprised of banks and investment houses brought together from different countries.

Eurodollars. U.S. currency held in European bank accounts, generally to be used in international transactions.

Eurocurrency. The same thing as Eurodollars, only not necessarily dollars; rather, any money deposited outside the country in which that currency is used (e.g., francs deposited in a London bank).

Swaps. Yet another of the creative ways financial wizards have come up with for raising capital. There are two basic kinds: interest rate and currency. Basically, swaps are just that—swapping one thing for another, like your Reggie Jackson card for my Catfish Hunter card. Swaps allow issuers to pay the lowest possible interest rate on a debt security and then exchange it for a preferred form of debt.

Cross Rate. The exchange rate between two different currencies. The dollar is used as middleman here. For example, when changing yen to German marks, the yen is first exchanged for dollars and then the marks are bought with those dollars.

BREAKING IN

In terms of jobs, experts seem to agree that there aren't too many spots abroad for Americans in the consumer end of banking. Banks have learned that it's usually wiser to hire a country's own, for the reasons cited earlier—the people's trust, understanding of cultural styles, and familiarity with laws and regulations. There are jobs for Americans, however, at the high-level end of loans and securities. John I. Banker (a fictitious name) is an international banker at one of the leading commercial banks. He is also in charge of recruitment, and observed the following about opportunities in international banking:

Q: What kind of opportunities are there in international banking for young people?
A: It's much more difficult than it used to be. First, commercial banking is in a down phase. It is shrinking and consolidating as banks are earning less. This makes a wide variety of general training difficult, and hiring at every bank is much less than before. It also is much more difficult to transition from trainee to vice president or financial advisor. So banks are changing hiring and contract patterns and are looking at young people as two- and three-year hirees. One

out of twenty young people will be asked to stay and the rest will be thanked for their time. Many will go to business school. Others will have to look for jobs.

Q: Is it important to go to business school?

A: It depends on the individual, in terms of maturity, knowledge, and marketing skills. B.A. candidates who can transition into an associate or vice president type of environment are rare. The MBA tends to be the entry ticket.

Q: And do you find that there are many MBAs who want to get into this area of the business?

A: We have the ability, like all banks, to pick from highly talented people. But we also have the same transition problem. There aren't as many twenty-eight-year-old MBAs around as there used to be. Now they are twenty-three or twenty-four. These younger people don't have the job experience that used to be traditional, and that hurts them. We do have an active recruiting program. We probably don't hire more than 25 or 30 out of 300 to 1,000 candidates.

Q: How attractive is fluency in a foreign language or having lived in another country?

A: Language fluency has very little value, since it is hard to match that language with a country you will want to work with. Experience in another country is not as important as it was because most banks are reducing their staffs abroad. [Author's note: Some other experts I spoke with do not agree. They feel that foreign language skills make a candidate much more attractive. Those who speak Japanese can be especially interesting to recruiters. As one put it, "If you speak Japanese you're as good as hired."]

Q: What about understanding a culture different from your own?

A: The only way that it is valuable is as a maturing process. The life spans of financial markets and products are so short that what used to be valuable to us isn't now.

Q: What are some of the things that you are looking for, in addition to maturity?

A: Some kind of work experience. It doesn't make a lot of difference what work that is. If I look at B.A. candidates who didn't work summers or have part-time jobs in college or never sold anything, the interviews will be very short. If they're looking for their first real job, I have no interest in them whatsoever.

Q: What if they were very active on campus, in student government or on the student newspaper or things like that?

A: It helps somewhat, but if they have no concept of what it takes to earn money or to work twelve hours a day or to work five or six days a week, they are high-risk candidates.

Q: Are you saying that it doesn't matter to you if they sold tires at a department store, that you simply want work experience of any kind?

A: I'm actually interested in people who carried newspapers when they were twelve years old or worked in a grocery store on the weekend. Or, in fact, had an after-school job doing anything. And selling is phenomenal. Anyone who has worked in a department store is phenomenal because he'll have met customers and know what it takes to push a product. Basically, bankers are salesmen.

I want indoor work experience, someone who has worked somewhere for a year or two. You look for people with leadership skills—president of the class, president of the student body, editor of the paper, things of that type. These people have shown some leadership qualities and have distinguished themselves from others. That can be important.

PROFILE: BARBARA S. THOMAS
SENIOR VICE PRESIDENT
IN CHARGE OF THE
INTERNATIONAL PRIVATE BANKING
DIVISION OF BANKERS TRUST

Meet an extraordinary woman—Barbara S. Thomas, who through intelligence, tenacity, and skill has positioned herself in a challenging and altogether fascinating job. Thomas's success story and her views serve as an inspiration to anyone who wants to enter the world of international banking.

In 1986, at the age of thirty-nine, Barbara Thomas was named a senior vice president and head of the international private banking division of Bankers Trust, the nation's seventh-largest commercial bank. This not inconsiderable achievement is only the most recent in a string of impressive professional moves.

After graduating from the University of Pennsylvania in 1966, at age nineteen, and NYU Law School three years later, Thomas was offered jobs where she would have been the first woman attorney on board. "When I started to work," she recalls, "there were very few women who had serious jobs anywhere. I wasn't very involved in whether I was the first woman or the second woman or the third woman. I took the position, and I believe it to this day, that the most important thing was for people to listen to what I said rather than just look at me.

"I wasn't planning to be a banker. I was planning to be a lawyer. I had the feeling that if you wanted to have a successful profession in the business world, you were better off being a lawyer than a banker, because lawyers really have a skill. If you have honed that skill so that it's very, very sharp, people will sort of be forced to listen to you because of your expertise. In my experience in those days, whether or not it was right or wrong, I thought bankers were more generalist. And once you were dealing with generalists, it was clear that there was no reason to hire a woman when you could have a man."

For a brief time, Thomas considered being a consumer lawyer and doing public work. Because of her interest in this area, she chose the large law firm Paul, Weiss, Rifkind, Wharton & Garrison, where it would be available to her. "My theory was, yes, you can be economically independent and work for a very good law firm. But you can also do pro bono work. The first work I did at Paul, Weiss was to help Charles Evers set up a fund to bring Northern white money down to very poor black communities in the South."

Somewhat to her surprise, Thomas discovered that corporate work caught her interest. First, she handled new issues, but when that line dried up in a market shift, she switched to mergers and acquisitions. She also left Paul, Weiss for the Park Avenue law firm of Kaye, Scholer, Fierman, Hays & Handler, where at age 30, she became a partner. After a few years of that, Thomas again got the itch to move on. Just at the point when she was seriously considering buying a business, President Carter put out the word that he wanted a woman on the Securities and Exchange Commission. This was in 1980. Since Thomas had good securities credentials and since there were few other qualified women, she

118

GETTING INTO MONEY

was selected for an interview. "I was so surprised by the whole thing," she remembers, "that I didn't believe it when one of my partners called and said he'd just gotten a call from the White House to say I was on a short list to be an SEC commissioner. I said, 'Look, Peter, I have to close this deal. I don't have time for your jokes.' And he said, 'It's not a joke.'" Then I said, 'You call back the White House and tell them I'll be very glad to come in for an interview.'"

Thomas was appointed a member of the Securities and Exchange Commission. She moved to Washington, D.C., where her husband, also a lawyer and a partner at Paul, Weiss, commuted on weekends from New York. That arrangement stayed in place for three years, until a baby and the chance to work as an investment banker in Hong Kong came along. The offer was from Samuel Montagu & Company, a London-based merchant bank. In contemplating this offer, Thomas was "intrigued with being their first woman board member." So the family settled in Hong Kong.

A merchant bank, as Barbara Thomas explains it, falls in between an American investment bank and an American commercial bank. Samuel Montagu didn't take deposits, but it did lend money. It also did project financing, loan indications, corporate finance (which was Thomas's area), trading, marketing, and investment management.

By 1986, Thomas and her husband felt it was time to head back to New York. Enter Bankers Trust and the position Barbara Thomas currently holds as head of the international private banking division. "Investment banking is really perfect for me," she says. "It's client-oriented, which is what my strength is. It's also about selling products, about marketing services that are legally based, that is to say, trust services and marketable instruments—stocks and bonds, investment management—which I learned a bit about when I was at Montagu's." In her current job, Thomas manages about 110 private bankers who are based all over the world, in Hong Kong, Singapore, London,

Switzerland, Miami, and New York. These people market the services the bank offers. Meanwhile, Thomas runs the operation. She oversees new products, hiring, the budget, and of course makes sure that profits are increasing. She also has kept her hand in marketing, particularly in Hong Kong, where she has excellent contacts.

According to Thomas, a typical transaction might be to assist a foreigner in investing his money. South Americans and Asians, she notes, are especially interested in investing outside their countries. Thomas's division works with both individuals and private companies, doing portfolio management with substantial amounts of money. The division sets up trusts and offshore corporations, and sells, finances, and manages real estate abroad. Acting as a total financial advisor, the bank provides services in buying and selling stocks and has a discount broker at its disposal. For the $2 million minimum clients invest, service, not surprisingly, is a high priority.

And, not surprisingly, Barbara Thomas works extremely hard at her job. In fact, when she left Samuel Montagu for Bankers Trust, the transition involved what was perhaps the most extraordinary commute ever heard of—from Hong Kong to New York. Thomas explains how she got into that situation: "When I began working [for Bankers Trust], we essentially agreed that I would take the job in July 1986 but start working in 1987. But once people get enthusiastic about things and get geared up to do them, they want to do them immediately. Once I started, I realized that it was a New York job. I couldn't stay on the phone. So I commuted from Hong Kong to New York about every other week or every third week." She credits the ability to sleep on airplanes as having gotten her through this commuting period.

Thomas's daily schedule is exhausting just to contemplate. It is also a monument to organization. Here's how one typical day goes: "At 7:30 tomorrow morning I will meet my secretary, and I will read the mail and dictate answers. At 8:00 I will meet with two division heads and go over the preliminary numbers for the budget. We'll do that for an hour and a half. Then I will meet with someone to talk about an employee who wants to leave but whom we want to stay. I have to talk to the division head, and then I have to talk to the employee. I will see a client from Europe for half an hour and see if I can get him to give us more business than he already does. Then I am having lunch with a more senior member of the bank from 12:30 to 2:00, since we will talk about marketing our services inside the bank. I want to get his division to recommend clients to us. Then from 2:00 to 6:00 I have one-hour meetings scheduled with each of my foreign division heads who are in town for the big budget meeting that will be the next day. At 6:30 I have an appointment with someone from the Metropolitan Museum of Art to talk about maybe having a function for our private clients at the museum. At 8:30 I have a business dinner with a man from Chicago who is interested in doing a real estate deal with us. Then I'll go home and talk to my secretary in Hong Kong who is set up to call me at 11:30. She'll read me the mail and tell me the telephone calls. At 12:15 I'll call my husband in Hong Kong, and hopefully go to bed at 12:30 or 1:00. That's tomorrow. The next day will be different, since we have budget meetings all day, starting at 7:30, and then I'm having all the division heads over for dinner so that we can keep talking."

When asked what keeps her going day after grueling day, Thomas replies, "Adrenaline. I'm very up about this. I think this is a terrific job, and I love it. And I want us to be way ahead of our budget by the end of [next year]."

Thomas also admits that the economical rewards for international bankers are satisfying. She's not allowed to talk specifics, but, she says, the pay is "good . . . not as good as in investment banking. It's probably not as good as being a senior partner in a law firm, but it's certainly respectable."

That, of course, refers to someone on Thomas's level. Men and women just starting out, according to Thomas, can expect to make "about one-third what they would in an investment bank." With investment bankers with MBAs starting in the $80,000 to $100,000 range, this means that international bankers can expect to begin at $25,000 to $35,000.

But Thomas is quick to point out that salaries tend to be higher at Bankers Trust than at other banks. "It's a higher paying bank all along the way," she notes. "That's because we don't think we're a commercial bank. We call ourselves a merchant bank. In a regular bank, the rewards are less. Now the hours are less, and the pressure is theoretically less. I don't believe that personally. I think that whenever you're in a job there's a lot of pressure, because the pressure is to succeed in whatever environment you are in. But historically, there has been less pressure in commercial banks than in investment banks, fewer financial rewards, and less time consumed."

But what does it take to be a successful international banker? "I've always thought that in a commercial bank you have to be very congenial. [As for me] one of the reasons that it was easy to get a job in a commercial bank was that they all wanted a securities person."

As for the recent changes in international banking, Barbara Thomas says: "You used to make money on assets; commercial banking used to make money on loans to people. When rates were reasonably lower for banks to borrow money and when people really paid back their loans, that was a pretty good business to be in. But when people weren't paying back their loans, and it cost a lot to borrow money from people, and you couldn't lend it out at a big enough margin, the asset-based business became a bad business. With the tremendous loans to underdeveloped countries that were not paid back, the banks' balance sheets took a beating. Meanwhile, the investment banks who were not lending money began to look very attractive. So everybody wants to be in a fee-based business where a fee is taken based on what they've done, a transaction rather than the amount. That's what has brought everybody together."

JAPAN: LAND OF THE RISING YEN

First it was cars and electronic equipment. Now it's financial services. Without a single sayonara, the Japanese have taken first place in commercial banking. Dai-Ichi Kangyo Bank has cut ahead of Citicorp for world dominance. Nipping at its heels are Fuji Bank, Sumitomo Bank, Mitsubishi Bank, Sanwa Bank, Mitsubishi Trust & Banking, Norinchukin Bank, and Industrial Bank of Japan. In the whole world, only France's Banque Nationale de Paris and Credit Agricole are in the running. No American bank other than Citicorp can even be found in the dust. Thomas Chandos, director of international capital markets at Kleinwort Benson Ltd., London's largest merchant bank, was quoted in *Fortune* (October 27, 1986) as saying, "Most of us should expect to see Japan as the dominant influence in the financial markets for the rest of our working lives."

How have the Japanese gotten such a stronghold on banking? For one thing, they are famous for high quality and productivity. They work hard and they see results. Also, they've developed strategies quite different from those of other countries. The Japanese offer irresistibly cheap services. They undercut almost everybody else by lending at extremely low rates and accepting a lower profit margin. For example, where a U.S. bank would insist on a half-percent margin, a Japanese bank is likely to accept an interest margin of one-quarter of a percentage point. Thailand is one country that found this out when, after a coup attempt threw it into debt, it went seeking a foreign loan in September 1985. While the rest of the world's banks dragged their heels, the Japanese boldly stepped forward and came up with 70 billion yen, making it the largest, lowest-rate Euroyen-denominated loan ever obtained by any country.

This is only one example of how the mighty Japanese are operating. Smart bankers, and for that matter, smart people involved in any aspect of the financial world, wake up every morning and ask, "What are the Japanese up to today?" Some

American firms have sent their own people to Japan's shores, not only to keep abreast of this question, but to actively engage in business on Japanese turf. It was towards the end of 1986 that the Tokyo Stock Exchange opened its doors to foreign membership. Merrill Lynch and Goldman, Sachs were the first Americans to walk in. Yet, in the brave new world of 24-hour global trading, there is one gap—120 minutes between the close of the New York stock market and the opening of Tokyo's. That's barely time for ambitious international money watchers to catch a catnap.

EXPLODING OPPORTUNITIES IN LONDON

On October 27, 1986, London's role as an international financial center received a boost like no other in the city's history. On that day, known as the Big Bang, deregulation hit the City of London (that city's equivalent of Wall Street). Because of that event, London has become, as one reporter put it, something akin to "a medieval market town for the global money merchants—the site where the key participants meet, compete, and exchange ideas." And not surprisingly, it's where foreign money merchants, including Americans, are flocking to set up shop.

A managing director of Salomon Brothers International Ltd. has called their London base "the flagship of our international operations." Goldman, Sachs International also sees London "as the place to be." These, along with Morgan Stanley, First Boston, and others who have been expanding their London bases, are, of course, investment banks, not commercial banks. But where one goes, so go the others. Citicorp Investment Bank, for example, has purchased two British brokerage houses, Scrimgeour Kemp-Gee and Vickers de Costa.

In the simplest terms, the Big Bang eliminated fixed commissions, something that occurred in the U.S. in 1975, thereby making commissions negotiable. Also dropped were the barriers that kept apart brokers, traders, merchant banks, and commercial banks, and discouraged foreign firms from operating out of London.

Worldwide competitive capital markets could not find a more suitably located heart than the City of London. It's a mere hop to Europe's world capitals and, thanks to the Concorde, not too much farther to New York. Tokyo is also quite reachable. For traders, the time schedule is ideal. Five hours ahead of New York, they can deal with our stock exchanges in the afternoon. Mornings are spent with Tokyo. And technology keeps everyone in touch.

It goes without saying that the lack of a language barrier is a real boon to U.S. banks, and that opportunities for Americans abound. The City has been and remains the center for Eurobond trading, and foreign currency trading is nearly double what's done in either New York or Tokyo. To handle these and other new opportunities that have opened up thanks to the Big Bang, American banks and brokerage houses have not only moved in their furniture but built their own houses.

The face of the City of London, located behind the majestic dome of St. Paul's Cathedral, has been rearranged as foreign firms add to the gene pool. And firms such as Citicorp and Salomon Brothers have stretched the boundaries of London's financial district by building in other sections. Citicorp's two new buildings can be reached by the ferry that's been set up to run every fifteen minutes. Morgan Stanley and Credit Suisse First Boston are part of a consortium that's settled on what used to be known as the Isle of Dogs, because this bit of dockland in London's East End once housed the royal kennels. Now known as Canary Wharf, it's a $2 billion complex that claims to be Europe's largest real estate complex. Obviously someone's got to fill these spaces.

The *New York Times* ran a chart a month before the Big Bang took effect that included figures on staff increases in preparation for life after October 27. Here, in part, is that list. The increases tell an obvious story about job opportunities.

AMERICAN COMPANY	LONDON EMPLOYEES	
	1984	1986
Bankers Trust	610	710
Chase Manhattan	1,407	2,480
Citicorp	1,350	2,100
Goldman, Sachs	140	500
Merrill Lynch	1,000	1,700
Morgan Stanley	124	600
Salomon Brothers	160	574
Security Pacific	347	1,500
Shearson/Lehman Brothers	275	1,200

These days when Big Ben chimes, its reverberations bounce off the ever-widening avenues of Wall Street.

C H A P T E R 8

VENTURE CAPITALISTS: MISSIONARIES FOR CAPITALISM

Think about the computer you use everyday for work and play. Think about the chocolate chocolate chip ice cream you consumed last night, and the running shoes you're now lacing up so you can burn off the ice cream. Think, for just one minute, about where these items came from.

It takes a lot of time and money for people with good ideas to develop their inspirations into profit-bearing products. Such familiar brand names as Nike, Apple, and Haagen-Dazs might never have existed without the entrepreneurs from whose fertile brains they sprang. And those good ideas might have remained only that without the aid of venture capitalists, the individuals and institutions that bankroll and nurture developing companies. Venture capital (which is exactly what it sounds like—providing capital for ventures) is a high risk–high gain business for those with good intuition, business smarts, and a strong stomach for uncertainty.

All is not ice cream in the land of venture capital. For every Haagen-Dazs that makes mountains out of vanilla beans, about four other grand schemes fail. Of the three million new businesses that have been born in the U.S. over the past five years, far fewer than one million have made it. But when they do, watch out. In 1976, for example, in a San Francisco tavern, venture capitalist Robert A. Swanson and University of California at San Francisco scientist Herbert W. Boyer agreed to form the first company to isolate and trick genes into reproducing the natural proteins needed for a new kind of medicine. They called their fledging biotechnology firm Genentech. Five years later, initial investments soared 800 times as supporters of Genentech happily watched the company go public. Genentech's is a story that venture capitalists turn to when they need a reminder of how right things can go.

Biotechnology, along with computers and other high-tech items, is the avenue many capitalists are venturing down these days. Genentech and Apple computers are only two of the companies that have benefited from being bankrolled. Nowhere in the world is venture capital action as heated as it is in the U.S.; and in the U.S., the hot spots are California's Silicon Valley and Boston's Route 128, where the majority of these firms have congregated. Of course, there are no geographic limitations to an entrepreneur's dreams, and work being funded by venture capitalists is being done all across the country—in Dallas, Denver, Colorado Springs, Champaign, and Baltimore. Most venture capitalists, though, like to stay close to the places they might or have put their money, so they, like the companies they back, have tended to gather around Boston and Silicon Valley. Always a draw, New York, too, attracts venture capitalists. Or is it that many of the capitalists who venture already are situated in New York?

HOW VENTURES AND CAPITALISTS GET TOGETHER AND WHERE THE MONEY COMES FROM

There is no lack of new ventures trying to get off the ground. Those that have needed a shot of capital have competed for the

attention of around 500 major venture capital firms and a lesser
number of individual venture capitalists. Lest you assume that
the firms have all that capital on hand, be advised they don't. A
part of the job is to raise a good chunk of the necessary money
from pension funds, financial institutions, and individuals. These
days, the foreign market is a likely place to look. "International
strategic partnering" is what it's often called. Japanese companies such as Nissan Motor Co., Nippon Steel Corp., and
Sumitomo Chemical Co. have become key allies of U.S. venture
capitalists. The Japanese, always competitive, seem to feel that
their investments will put them on the cutting edge of U.S.
technology, as well as make them money. Europeans have been
getting in on the action, too. Of the $2.3 billion committed by
U.S. venture capital funds in 1985, foreign investors contributed
24 percent, up from 8 percent of $661 million in 1980.

Another relatively new source of funding is colleges and universities. Schools see venture capital as a way to help fill their
coffers. Some colleges have set up industrial parks, established
facilities to incubate high-tech startups, and hired attorneys to
seek patents. Washington University in St. Louis has gone one
step further. On July 18, 1986, the school announced a ten-year
agreement with Alafi Capital Co., a Berkeley, California venture
capital firm, to put a venture capitalist on campus. The venture
capitalist is working alongside the School of Medicine to launch
biotechnical and biomedical research companies. The school and
Alafi are 50–50 partners in what's being called A/W Co., with
Alafi responsible for managing and financing the venture. How
did this seemingly unlikely marriage of business and academia
come about? Well, Monsanto happens to be a big-time sponsor
of Washington University, having committed to a ten-year, $52
million research arrangement. Monsanto also happens to be the
major investor in Alafi. That's how the initial introductions between the school and Alafi were made . . . not entirely altruisti-
cally. A Monsanto-funded research project was the first to be
spun into a company.

State government is another place venture capitalists are starting to go for money. Traditionally, state pension funds haven't been allowed to take a piece of the action when they invest, and this obviously has deterred their interest. But increasingly, prohibitions are being lifted. Michigan was a frontrunner when in 1982 the legislature passed a law allowing state pension funds to invest in new Michigan businesses and to participate in venture partnerships in and out of the state. The Michigan Venture Capital Fund has been followed by Ohio's Thomas Edison Program and the Illinois Development Finance Authority. All three are, of course, helping to pull the notion of venture capital into the heartland from its Northeast and West Coast centers. Connecticut and Colorado have also gotten into the game, with, no doubt, other states at least considering it.

There are individuals who sink their cash into new ventures. Sometimes they catch up with each other at one of the venture capital clubs that have been meeting for the last couple of years. The clubs host luncheons where entrepreneurs pitch their "must do's" to investors with $10,000 and up.

Although it's really only in the last ten years that venture capital has become one of the glamour areas, the field has a venerable history. Henry Ford and Andrew Carnegie might never have introduced their products without financial aid. The telephone might never have rung and the light bulb might never have been lit had the inventions of Alexander Graham Bell and Thomas Edison been unable to find funding. And wealthy gentlemen might have had to make do with less if they had been too shortsighted to see and profit from the future—John Jay Whitney, for example, who backed what became Minute Maid orange juice.

These days a new breed, such as Pittsburgh billionaire Henry Hillman, is helping to keep America on the move. Hillman, reputedly an extremely private, behind-the-scenes kind of man ("The whale only gets harpooned when he spouts" is his company's

informal motto), has bankrolled a diverse group of companies—
everything from Hybritech Corp. of San Diego, a genetic-engi-
neering concern, to Kohlberg, Kravis & Roberts, the dynamo
New York investment firm that popularized the leveraged buyout. Hillman's low-key approach doesn't mean he's a small-time
player by any means. By one account, Hillman holds at least a
20 percent equity stake in eighty-four separate companies. His
first venture capital investment, in the early 1970s, in the San
Francisco-based venture capital firm Kleiner, Perkins, Caufield
& Byers (now one of the heavy hitters) was described by
Kleiner Perkins cofounder Thomas J. Perkins as "almost an
incidental investment [to Hillman]. It was like a missing item on
his checklist." The investment was $4 million.

Wealthy individuals are not the only people making important
contributions. Young people who work for venture capital firms
are fast becoming indispensable to the business. They are, in
fact, so attractive, that *Time* (June 16, 1986) featured four young
stars in its article on venture capital. They were:

John Doerr—Described as "a relentless overachiever,"
Doerr joined the San Francisco venture capital firm of Kleiner,
Perkins, Caufield & Byers when he was twenty-eight and became one of five general partners (now there are seven) when
he was thirty-one. His field is computers, and it is estimated that
the companies he has picked have earned $260 million in ven-
ture profits.

Jennifer Lobo—In 1985, at age thirty, Lobo helped found the
Princeton, New Jersey-based venture capital firm Domain Associates, where she now works fourteen- to eighteen-hour days
handling health care ventures. That's not the first "founding"
she's done. Ohio's Standard Oil recruited her at an earlier time
to help start up Vista Ventures, located in New Canaan, Connecticut.

Bryan Cressey—Cressey also started his own venture capital firm, Golder, Thoma & Cressey, in 1980, when he was thirty. The initial $60 million startup money for the Chicago company ballooned in six years to two funds worth $160 million. Cressey "rides herd on nine companies, primarily in the health care industry," says *Time.* He describes his life as a venture capitalist as "addictive."

David Croll—Croll started out at the Bank of Boston, but three years later joined Boston's TA Associates, where he is now a managing partner. It was in 1979, when Croll was thirty, that he teamed up with entrepreneur Steven Dodge, using TA's money and strategic guidance to help Dodge catapult his American Cablesystems into a $200 million plus business. Meanwhile, Croll became TA's communications specialist.

WHAT IT TAKES

Three of the four young venture capitalists highlighted in *Time* first received degrees in non-business areas before switching over. They've used these early interests and training to segue into their current positions. John Doerr, the computer man, got his master's in electrical engineering at Houston's Rice University. Jennifer Lobo, the health care specialist, explored her love of microbiology at the University of California at Berkeley. David Croll, communications expert, studied engineering at Cornell University.

Only Bryan Cressey, who like Lobo covers health care, had his sights set on venture capital from the start. His combined law and business degrees from Harvard set him on that path after graduation in 1976. Even with such impressive degrees and a focused approach, it was difficult for him at that time to find a job. The venture capital field has revved up quite a bit since 1976 and opportunities now, by comparison, abound, but the point is still well taken that it's sometimes best to enter a field such as this one from an angle of interest in the product.

Cressey isn't the only one to have honed his talents with an MBA. Doerr and Croll also picked up business degrees at Harvard. Lobo went to the University of Chicago for her MBA. As in most areas of Wall Street, those three little letters are crucial to landing a top-of-the-line job.

It also doesn't hurt to have shown creativity and ambition right from the start. When John Doerr was only a sophomore, he started a computer software company. Later, during his Harvard days, he worked part-time at Intel, the semiconductor firm. You can be sure that his drive, in addition to the experience he gained, won him points during job interviews.

What does it take to be successful at venture capital? Perhaps the most important skill is, as one venture capitalist suggests, "a nose for success." What he means is that without the ability to pick ventures that are going to grow and show a profit, you're out of business. "The nose," of course, works in tandem with the ability to take a good, pragmatic look at the entrepreneur's plans, setup, and management capabilities. Stanley Golder, a partner in the Chicago firm of Golder, Thoma & Cressey, reported that his group studied 1,200 deals in 1985 . . . out of which they chose six.

Once your enthusiasm has been fired up, you might have to search out funding (as discussed in the previous section) or convince your colleagues. This is the part of the job where salesmanship comes in. Later, when the project is underway, you probably will have to change hats again and become a manager. And possibly a heavyweight manager, at that. With so much invested in risky businesses, venture capitalists can ill afford to play "Mr. Nice Guy." At best, you'll provide advice in the areas of management, operations, finance, and marketing. At worst, you'll have to replace people—maybe even the entrepreneur whose original concept is moving from abstraction to reality. It has been estimated that before they reach maturity, somewhere around 50 percent to 60 percent of all venture-backed companies see changes in key personnel. Needless to say, this can be rough for both the company and the venture capitalist. But for the tough-minded who can live with the uncertainty of helping birth an idea and see it grow, venture capital is the way to go. As they say, "Nothing ventured, nothing gained."

FRED ADLER
VENTURE CAPITALIST

Frederick R. Adler has a reputation as a tough customer. At sixty-three, Adler has been down the pike more than once, and what he appreciates, or rather demands, according to most reports, is performance. Adler, who manages somewhere around $185 million in venture capital funds, is best known for picking winners such as Data General Corp. and Fibronics International Inc.

As for his style, Business Week (September 1, 1986) noted: " . . . Adler is known as a strong-willed, domineering investor *who favors close control." The* Wall Street Journal *(August 22, 1986) pretty much concurred with this assessment. They reported that Adler "has . . . developed a reputation as an impatient and volatile investor who doesn't tolerate dissent. . . . Indeed, when investments go sour, Mr. Adler is famous for the speed with which he boots lax managers." In his own defense, Adler responded: "I don't think our investors give us a management fee and a 20 percent share of the profits to be passive investors. If the management cannot manage effectively, you have to bring in those who can."*

When asked more recently what he thought of these articles, Adler had this to say: "The tough guy impression of these articles is nonsense. I probably act too slowly rather than too quickly, I try to make changes as a gentleman, without abuse, and frequently help find new jobs for the managers involved. In any event, the facts prove the correctness of the actions taken. The dismissed CEO of the largest company referred to in the articles joined Adler & Co. after resigning, and then founded a new company and requested us to lead the new financing, which we did. The second company was on the edge of bankruptcy, and was salvaged over the next six months by an Adler & Co. team which then nogotiated a merger with a larger, profitable company. The third was losing both money and market share. We reduced costs and brought in a new manager. It is now quite profitable."

One of several offices this complex businessman uses is on the forty-second floor of a monolithic Park Avenue tower. Perhaps the height and the view remind him of American business's vast possibilities. As for the office itself, it defies the traditional executive image. While well appointed, a pink paper airplane rests on the rust colored carpet. There are two stamps on the desk: one says "Brilliant"; the other has a question mark. There is a ceramic ashtray with the words "I love you." A plaque reminds us that "there is no limit to what a man can do or where he can go if he doesn't mind who gets the credit."

Behind the desk littered with mementos sits Fred Adler himself,

*a trim, blond man, primed for action. His eyes, crinkly and blue,
are shrewd.*

Q: I am a little confused about the two offices you have.
Can you explain that?

A: I go back and forth to avoid wasting time on useless
meetings. I have meetings in both places, back and forth,
frequently in other people's offices. It is a very informal system. My leveraged buyout firm has a third office across the
street, too, which I do not use. Adler & Shaykin on the
fourteenth floor. Adler & Co. is on the thirty-third floor, and R
& M [Reavis & McGrath], of which I'm still a senior partner, is
here. So I just do whatever I think makes sense. And occasionally I start the day by having breakfast appointments, if I'm in
New York, in our New York pied-à-terre, and even on days
when I have all my appointments in New Jersey in my home.

Q: Why do you do this?

A: Well, because whatever's most efficient. I don't want to
feel locked in anywhere. Should I? The point is to get the
work done in the most effective manner. Last Wednesday
night I flew to Paris on the Concorde, got up for a breakfast
due diligence meeting at the Ritz on Thursday morning for
one of our portfolio companies. After it was over had another
meeting and worked out in my room for an hour. Then I went
to a lunch due diligence meeting, then had another afternoon
meeting, and then flew to London on the 5:30, caught the 7:15
Concorde, got back to New York at 6:00 for a dinner at 7:30,
then I went home.

Q: Were you tired?

A: Not really. And on Sunday I took the 4:00 P.M. flight out
of Newark, landed in San Francisco, had three meetings at
the San Francisco airport that evening, three meetings the
next day in San Francisco and caught the 3:00 back.

Q: What keeps you going?

A: Probably I am somewhat neurotic. I find business both exciting and amusing.

Q: Then I take it you like what you're doing.

A: Yes.

Q: Tell me more about what you do.

A: I do a variety of things. I make paper airplanes. There is one over there. I shoot rubber bands. Seriously, though, we have a venture capital firm which is fair-sized. I think I'm reasonably well known as a venture capitalist. I think if you check you'll find that some people like me, some people don't like me. Some of them will tell you that I can be tough, occasionally confrontational. While I don't think of myself as particularly difficult, I tend to be very direct and I sometimes tend to dominate meetings when companies are in deep trouble. If a company is in danger, I feel I have to move rapidly to be quick on the trigger if, if necessary, to take real steps to solve the problems before the company goes under.

Q: Do you think these attributes are typical of venture capitalists? Or do you think you are unique?

A: I have no idea whether it's typical for other people. [Venture capitalists] vary a lot. There's nothing typical about anybody. I think the only thing that's typical of the more experienced, more highly regarded venture capitalists is their dedication to doing the right thing.

Q: What do you mean by "the right thing"?

A: Trying to straighten out the companies in which they are involved. If they're public firms, make them work so that the public doesn't take a bath in the public offering. I like to think that it's typical of the better venture capitalists, the people who have been in the field for ten years or more, that they have an image of themselves that includes a sense of responsibility. That includes Peter Crisp, Benno Schmidt, Tom Perkins. They're all of a type. They all have an inordinate sense of responsibility. They have a great deal of pride in their reputations. They have a feeling that they have to work more than is necessary to make the company they are involved with work, if at all possible. And they get very upset, not so much at losing as at the feeling that they are not doing the job right. What bothers me the most is when I'm not doing the job right.

Q: Why does it bother you?

A: Because whatever goes wrong in a company in which I'm actively involved is my fault. I should have picked it up. I just misread the people or the technology or the market. Or, after I invested in it, I misread the situation and failed to make compensating changes, or if I wasn't able to sway management, I failed in my powers of persuasion.

Q: Do you think about the larger issue of how you are affecting the American economy?

A: That's the smaller issue. As long as you build the company's profits, you will help the economy. That's by definition. You don't have to worry about that. I don't make enough out of venture capitalism alone to justify the seventy hours of weekly time commitment I give it. I can make as much or more out of buying into larger companies and helping their experienced managements.

Q: Are you involved in buyouts as well?

A: Yes, absolutely, although the great bulk of my time is spent on venture capital. Shaykin bought the *Chicago Sun Times.* We have the largest maker of prison locks in the world. We have an outdoor advertising company that we bought in the Southeastern United States. We control one of the largest manufacturers of mining equipment. We have all sorts of companies, big and small.

Q: Diverse.
A: And very profitable.

Q: How did you get into this?
A: I went to Harvard Law School on a scholarship, for which I'm forever grateful to Harvard.

Q: Where did you do your undergraduate?
A: I went to North Carolina State for a few months, while I was in the Army. And then I went to Brooklyn College for two and one-half years. And then from Harvard Law School I went to a law firm, and while I was in the law firm I became a trial lawyer. Then in 1959, through a combination of (a) an accident, and (b) a big mouth, I became president of a small publicly owned company on the edge of insolvency. I helped turn it around. It, in turn, became involved in a leveraged buyout of something else. I had the fun of doing that and found that I liked business. It was a fairly rational and commonsense thing. It seemed to me rather simple. I could understand what people were talking about. Invariably, [when I don't understand what people are saying] it means that there is some simple solution that they are missing.

Q: So you are looking for the reduction. You are looking for the core.
A: Remember William of Ockham at the time of Bacon? He was a friar in England who was a philosopher. And he believed that what you do is strip off all the fat and get to the muscle, the core of each question. Really what you do is cut through the mass of peripheral matter and get to the few core elements of each thing. Even the peripheral matters have core elements.

Q: What do you say to young people who are interested in venture capital?

A: Get some operating experience.

Q: What do you mean by operating experience?

A: Go through a training program with IBM or General Electric. Get your hands dirty working on a project. That's what really counts. And follow this up by thinking about why other people do things. What is their psychology? What is their reason for doing things? And then listen to Kenny Rogers' song "The Gambler." A perfect song for a venture capitalist. And yet, it's not a gamble at all.

Q: I wanted to ask you about the risk.

A: Well, depending on what you do, the risk is high on any one deal. But if you diversify properly in different channels of investment, then you're going to come out all right. Particularly if you watch the companies and work like hell with the management to teach the people to become their own management consultants. Over a period of time teach them, and then they don't need you anymore. The ultimate leverage in my business, even though my reputation is to be a manager, is to let someone else manage it. You don't have to manage. A venture capitalist who acts as a temporary manager is like a fireman. You're responding to an emergency situation and when it's finished, you should get out. The ultimate use of power is to get rid of it. Let someone else take the job. I'd rather make my money by somebody else doing the job. There are only so many jobs I can do.

Q: How much of a watchdog are you?

A: I watch most everything. Unfortunately, paranoia in business is reality.

Q: Do you ever find that tough or distasteful?

A: Whether it is distasteful to me is irrelevant. It's a fact of life. There's nothing I can do about it.

Q: Was there a time when you found it tough, or have you always liked business?

A: Sure, sometimes, I find it very tough, very time consuming, and I get very tired. But not being busy is worse. Like many people I probably expect more of myself than I am capable of doing. If things are easy, I become bored, and I deliberately take on too much. Then I get in trouble again.

Q: Well, if it's what you like . . .

A: I like working. I really believe in venture capitalists. And not just me. I'm just one. I think there are better guys in this business. Whatever their motives, whether they're suspect or confused, whether it's money or self-satisfaction or self-image or ego or power, the country gets a tremendous edge. On a commonsense basis, I'd say overall that what I do is good.

HAMBRECHT & QUIST:
A SAN FRANCISCO SUCCESS STORY

Three-thousand miles from Fred Adler's offices, in San Francisco, is the headquarters of another extremely interesting and profitable company that, it is no exaggeration to say, has its eye on the future. Because Hambrecht & Quist is one of the leading investment banking and venture capital firms in the United States and because its bases (in addition to San Francisco, the firm has offices in Boston, New York, Los Angeles, Menlo Park, and London) are widely spread, it is well worth taking a look at.

Venture capital was the original focus of Hambrecht & Quist

when it was founded in 1968 by William Hambrecht and George Quist. The two men were venture capitalists working respectively for F. I. Dupont (which has since gone out of business) and Bank of America. Both were having trouble getting their bosses interested in financing emerging businesses; they also were frustrated by the red tape wrapped around their deals. So they raised some capital for their own venture and started Hambrecht & Quist. Bill Hambrecht, today recognized as a premier venture investor, remains as president and co-chief executive officer.

Although H&Q's activities have expanded to include corporate finance, trading and research, venture capital remains the front end of the business. Specializing in technology, health care, and other emerging growth companies, H&Q has been involved with some of those fields' biggest success stories—Compaq, Lotus, Apple, and Genentech among them.

H&Q's chairman and co-chief executive officer Gordon S. Macklin underscores the importance of the venture capital part of the business when he notes that, although all of his company's areas are integrated and rely on each other, "the opportunity to

Gordon S. Macklin

hit an out-of-the-park home run has to be in the venture area."
Here is an example that Macklin gives of a whopping home run:
A few years back, H&Q committed "a couple of million dollars
in financing to some guys who came out of Xerox with an idea
for desktop publishing." The scientists had no real experience
in operating a business, so Hambrecht & Quist, along with the
capital it provided, came in with their business startup know-
how. Together they started a company to do the software for
this publishing venture. Well, it worked out so well that they got
additional financing from Apple and others, and today that company—Adobe—has a capitalized value in excess of $300 million.
"Those home runs don't happen often," admits Gordon Macklin.
But of course they are what any venture capitalist tries to hit.

While H&Q specializes in Adobe-type ventures, they occasionally are lured by flashier ideas. They have, for example,
invested in Samuel Adams Beer, "the Dove Bar of bottled beer,"
as Macklin describes it. Aimed at young professionals, it is made
only with the finest ingredients. As with all of their involve-
ments, H&Q hopes that Samuel Adams Beer will catch on in a
big way. "Our culture," says Macklin, "is 'Growth investments
for growth investors.' "

In addition to its work with what is called "value-added startups," such as Adobe and Samuel Adams Beer, H&Q has developed another profitable area of business—turnarounds. Macklin
describes these as "companies that are not well. As a matter of
fact, by the time they get to the turnaround group, they're
somewhere between intensive care and pathology." In these
cases, H&Q specialists go in and operate, nursing the company
back to health, and where necessary removing the diseased area
by changing management.

As for the investment banking arm of Hambrecht & Quist, it
evolved quite organically. After getting companies started and
working with them to become successful, offering them investment banking services was a natural next step. Says Macklin on
the subject of this expansion, "In order to see the widest variety

of venture opportunities, our firm believes you should offer the whole package of services." Actually, Gordon Macklin, who came to H&Q in 1987, is himself proof of H&Q's ever-growing commitment to teaming venture capital with investment banking.

Before joining Hambrecht & Quist in 1987, Macklin was for seventeen years president of the National Association of Securities Dealers (NASD), where, among other achievements, he helped introduce the automated quotations systems (NASDAQ) that brought order to the over-the-counter (OTC) market. It is largely due to his leadership that the NASD is now the third-largest trading market in the world. Previous to his term at the NASD, Macklin was with the Cleveland securities firm McDonald & Co. for twenty years. With this background, he has obviously brought solid investment banking knowledge with him to Hambrecht & Quist.

This is fortunate, because in recent years the competition has gotten much stiffer. Back when H&Q first started, you could say that they owned the bat, the ball, and the field, meaning it was relatively natural for a company that had been nurtured by H&Q to stay with them when it came time to go public. But these days a venture capital relationship is no longer a guarantee of later loyalty. While 70 percent to 80 percent of the companies H&Q helps start up stay with them for their investment banking needs, the other 20 percent to 30 percent jump ship. Plus many of the major investment banks have opened their own venture capital departments as a way to get in on the ground floor and "buy" the public offering business that comes later.

What this means is that while the ambiance at Hambrecht & Quist may be of the relaxed variety the West Coast is famous for, the workload is straight Wall Street. Seventy-hour workweeks are common for everyone. But so are opportunities. Undergraduates, working primarily on the public side of the business, develop their skills on the job and work their way up the ladder. Analysts are often brought in after working in their field of expertise. MBA candidates are recruited for the corporate finance department. The venture capital group is a broad mix of people who come with operating experience in the technologies. Some have come from the public side of the business, where a combination of corporate finance and/or research, plus the building of their skills, has led them in the direction of small, private companies.

Once you've got a foot in the door, there's room to move. One employee, for example, was transferred from health care research to the venture group after, in the course of her work, she brought in four health care-related venture investments. Looking at geographic distribution, the bulk of the crew—about 200—is in the San Francisco office. Approximately 65 work out of New York, with 15 or so each in Boston, Los Angeles, and London. By and large it's a youngish group. Macklin puts the average age at "just south of forty."

Macklin sums things up this way: "Functionally, there are many, many ties between venture, research, and corporate finance. In some ways, if you want to stand back and take a simplistic look at this business, it could look just like Lazarus. These people buy the merchandise and these people sell the merchandise. There is a melded function there, and many career opportunities between the three.

"We think [what we're doing] is best described as merchant banking. If you're with a merchant bank on the buying side of the business, you are at or near a venture career."

CHAPTER 9

ECONOMISTS AND ANALYSTS: BACK TO THE FUTURE

"**I**f we knew where the market was going, we'd all be rich," is an age-old Wall Street lament. But then, uncertainty is the name of the investment game, and trying to outsmart the ups and downs is what keeps people playing. Investors always welcome a little advice from the sidelines, and that's where analysts and economists come in.

Analysts are something like the studio audience on "Let's Make a Deal," encouraging you to pick either Door Number One or the large box because they think they know which holds the big prize. Of course analysts' decisions are based on more than gut instinct; their recommendations are backed up with solid research. The analyst's job is to know everything about an industry and keep abreast of all new developments, to apply that information to an overall knowledge of how the stock market works, and synthesize everything to form solid buy-and-sell predictions that make money for clients.

Wall Street economists do somewhat the same thing as analysts, except instead of directing decisions within a particular market, they study the economic conditions that influence the entire scene. In other words, analysts study the micro picture, while economists tackle the macro.

THE ANALYST'S LIFE

Being an analyst is considered one of the more glamorous
Wall Street jobs. The glamour aspect, in addition to excellent
pay (easily six figures and known to go as high as a million
with investment banking input), is power. As one top analyst
says, "When I shake the tree, the apples fall," meaning that
his recommendation moves a stock price up or down, depending on his opinion. Plus, your clients actually listen to
you and follow your advice. They are, you might say, your
fan club.

Generally, analysts concentrate on a particular industry. It
could be aerospace or the auto industry, cosmetics or the stock
market itself. The analyst game gets into some pretty interesting areas, too: "leisure time," for example, and pollution control.
The analyst gleans as much information as possible about what
is to be covered and then synthesizes that information into
market predictions. The challenge is to understand a field from
top to bottom and make predictions to the institutional investor
clients that are more often accurate than not. Because these
clients are moving large amounts of capital, they probably have
little patience with an analyst who can't provide on-target advice. It would be fair to say then that the analyst's seat is a hot
one.

Ask one top analyst about the job and here's what you'll hear:
"Glamorous? Yes and no. There's a lot of drudge work. You
spend a lot of time going through numbers, financial data, trying
to get an edge on your competition, and then writing about it.
There's pressure to be first and to do a quality job, not just to
crunch numbers, and to get information out to your clients.
That's plain hard work. The glamorous aspect comes in when
you reach the point where you're recognized by the other top
analysts in your specific industry on the Street, and also by
clients. When you're on the road and people want to talk to you
because they know who you are, that's where the glamour

comes in. And when your ideas work out, that's particularly rewarding . . . when you actually make money for people."

What's it take to be a good analyst? For one thing, you have to have incredible stamina. Brenda Davis McCoy, a securities analyst covering the brokerage companies for PaineWebber, can attest to that. McCoy works seven days a week, and on those rare days when she doesn't come into the office, she brings work home with her. Waking up between 5 and 6 A.M., she reads the major newspapers before arriving at her office around 8:00. Often she doesn't leave until 9 or 10 at night. Her diet consists of junk food and Lean Cuisine. Yet when the pace finally catches up with her, McCoy has to force herself to take a break. That's because she loves what she does; what might seem like a torturous schedule to someone else is fun and rewarding to her.

"I know that the work sounds very, very hard," says McCoy, "but there are several things that are gratifying about it." You are, she emphasizes, in the business of making money for people. When her clients take huge positions, which, on the basis of McCoy's recommendations, afford them huge profits, she justifiably feels that "there's something very exciting about that."

To make it as an analyst you have to be able to wear several different hats. First, you need to be a good researcher. Second, you have to be able to synthesize those ideas in the reports you write. Finally, you have to have terrific sales skills. And, of course, a nose for picking stocks is crucial. As McCoy pragmatically points out, "Ultimately what counts in the research area is your ability to identify companies that are going to generate high levels of earnings in future years and stocks that are going to go up."

The office of another Brenda—Brenda Lee Landry, a securities analyst at Morgan Stanley who covers cosmetics, photography, and household items (like soap and perfume)—is a perfect example of how an analyst works. Binders of reports Landry has written, one for each company she covers, run along an entire

Brenda Lee Landry

wall of her office. Numerous reports are filed in each binder. Her office is neat and organized, but lest you get too carried away with the impression of total control, Landry will laughingly sweep back her chair and present the stacks of magazines she has stashed under her desk. Her bedroom, she claims, has even more piles. She spends her evenings reading all the publications she can get her hands on, everything from *Forbes* and *Business Week* to *Women's Wear Daily* and *Vogue* to *Advertising Age* and *Ad Week* to technical journals such as *Japan Trade News* and *Cosmetic World News.*

But reading isn't the only way the two Brendas and their associates gather information. Analysts also investigate. Like the best sleuths, they talk to the people who work in the industries they cover, from the CEO to the stock clerk. They visit shops and warehouses, inspecting the corners for dirt of the literal and figurative kind, searching out details that would indicate where a company stands. They try to find out the effect of the latest pending legal suit, the new financing, the newly appointed manager. When all is said and done, analysts are serious information people who work at staying highly conversant in their field of specialty. A successful auto industry analyst will know GM down to its door handles and spark plugs.

What happens to all this information? It gets presented to the investors who are, and who you hope will remain, your clients. That's where the sales side of being an analyst comes in. According to a survey by *Wall Street Letter,* the average analyst who used to spend about 70 percent of his time doing fundamental research now spends 45 percent of his time drumming up or keeping clients, cutting back research time by 15 percent or more. While marketing has always been a necessary evil, the competitive edge has gotten sharper. In an effort to keep the customer satisfied, some firms have installed client contact quotas. Even where quotas do not exist, there is new pressure to keep those fresh analyses coming. This means more reports to write and more telephoning and more personal contact, which means more time on the road—a lot more time. Most analysts spend about 25 percent of their time traveling.

One way of cutting down on client visits is the roadshow. This is where an analyst will make a presentation to a group. Brenda Landry is an expert at the roadshow. She will, for example, give a lunch for thirty-five institutions, regaling them between soup and nuts with stories, teaching them more about the industry and what they should be looking for, putting out her opinions based on her research, and raising such broad questions as whether they should be in the consumer area altogether or even, for that matter, in the stock market. Ideally, at the conclusion, they are impressed enough to follow her anywhere.

All of it—research, writing, presentations—is directed to one end: determining whether clients should be buying or selling certain stocks. What starts out as "best guessing" quickly becomes factual and concrete because your clients either make money or lose money based on your recommendations. You're either right or you're wrong. It's that simple. And that tough.

THE CREATIVE SIDE OF ANALYZING

Many of the 4,000 analysts who work for brokerage firms play
it safe, making noncontroversial forecasts that don't rock the
boat. They base their decisions on the facts and only the facts.
But the best and the brightest, and ultimately the most successful, don't simply juggle the numbers to come up with another
ho-hum prediction. They're much more creative personalities
than that.

Brenda Lee Landry's particular approach is almost sociologi-
cal. Landry finds it fascinating to fantasize about the products
and companies she covers. "I'll think, 'What would I do if I were
running this company?'" she says. "I love the puzzle of business, the question of how you survive in today's world." For
Landry, being an analyst is not just facts and figures, but also
an intellectual exercise. She compares it to playing chess. "What
makes the consumer tick?" she asks herself. "How is the consumer changing? What would my next move be?" To get the
answers, she studies ads and is always interested in talking to
people and hearing their views. She also tests new products, be
it a new shampoo that finds its way into her shower or a new
room deodorizer she sprays in her office.

When Kodak batteries were first introduced, for example, she
studied and studied the packaging. Was the black-and-gold color
scheme the most salable? she wondered. Or would Kodak have
been better off sticking with the yellow that is their trademark?
By diligently analyzing her products, Brenda Landry learns
when a company is right on the consumers' pulse and when it
has fallen off and can't find the beat any longer. Her track record
attests to the fact that her methods work. Landry's been an
analyst since 1970; burnout hasn't singed her yet. On the contrary, her energy and enthusiasm never seem to flag.

If you ask Landry what it takes to be a good analyst, she'll say,
"Imagination." By this she means being able to psych out a
situation, to read between the lines and hear what's *not* being

said, to use the ability to interpret information and come up with an accurate forecast. Yet something else Landry says also indicates why she's successful. "I hate to lose money. I can't stand to lose money."

THE ALL-AMERICA RESEARCH TEAM

Each year, the October issue of *Institutional Investor* ranks the top brokerage analysts for the preceding twelve months. Since the clients themselves do the voting, along with other analysts at top institutions and a sampling of portfolio managers, it goes without saying that it's great for your career to appear on the list. The awards cover about sixty-five industry headings and investment specialties, from aerospace to small growth companies, with first-, second-, and third-place winners and runners-up. If you're considering a career in research, don't miss this issue of *Institutional Investor.* No one in the business does.

THE DEAN OF WALL STREET

There's a securities analyst covering the brokerage field with the interesting moniker of "The Dean of Wall Street." It's a title well earned. Perrin Long's been at this business longer than just about anyone. In fact, he's responsible for introducing written reports to the industry. "No one was writing reports when I started writing reports," he recalls. "Back in 1976 it was just myself . . . covering the brokerage firms. I was sitting around one Sunday, reading an annual report from Merrill Lynch, so I wrote a report on Merrill and sent it back to the company and let them read it." After some go around, it was decided that Long's report would be sent to customers as a service. Out it went to about 3,000 institutional investors, but demand was so great that within six months another 60,000 copies had been printed and mailed. This is how Long realized he was onto something.

Perrin Long is an original in more ways than one. In his cramped office at Lipper Analytical Securities Corp. where he's a consultant ("It's where I hang my hat"), Long sits twinkly-eyed, puffing on a pipe. He's as likely to pull out a piece of string and perform a magic trick as he is to slip in some pearl of wisdom about his profession. A framed bit of needlework on his wall reads "Goodness is the only investment that never fails."

Here are some other Longisms on the nature of the research business:

"Most analysts work long hours to try to find that little hidden thing within the companies they follow that will set them apart, relative to their competitors, with their customers."

"[The job of analyzing the brokerage business] is highly cyclical. It goes up and down like a yo-yo. You cannot plan for the future. How can you plan for the future when you don't know where the market's going to be?"

"There are the people who manage money and there are the analysts. Basically, the people who manage want two things: (1) They want somebody to hold their hand; and (2) they want something in their files to justify why they did something."

"You write these reports and mail them to people who pay you for them. They read them, and hopefully you give them ideas. If you are successful [at] making money for people, they will come back to you looking for you to make them more money, to give them more ideas."

"[The hectic pace] can be very enjoyable. I started off last Wednesday at 7:00 at LaGuardia, flew to Chicago, saw four institutional clients and had lunch with one of them. I caught the 3:05 flight from Chicago to San Francisco, got into San Francisco around 5:00, went out with a client for dinner. I saw six or seven clients in San Francisco on Thursday. Then my wife joined up with me, having come from Los Angeles where she was on business. We had dinner with friends on Thursday night. I drove down to San Jose to see the city treasurer of San Jose. We called it quits at noontime on Friday and drove up to Napa Valley to the wine country and spent the night there. On Saturday morning we drove to Calistoga and took the mud baths and massages at 8 A.M. We were out of there by 10:15. We drove back to San Francisco, caught the 12:30 flight and got home Saturday night around 10:15."

"If we enjoy what we are doing, most of us will do it to excess."

"Once anybody gets hooked on the securities business, they stay hooked on it. When you're away, you always want to know what the market's doing. You would like to get a copy of the *New York Times* or the *Wall Street Journal,* so you can keep track of what's going on. Because you must remember that what the stock market does is cater to everybody's desire to gamble. The stock market is the largest form of legalized gambling in the world."

"The interesting thing about the securities business is that anybody who wants to work in it and has a little bit of luck can make more money in a short period of time than in any other business."

BREAKING IN

While analysts agree that an MBA is useful for breaking into the field, none of the three professionals highlighted in this chapter has the magic degree and they certainly haven't been held back.

Perrin Long, the senior member of the triumvirate, started as a $25-a-week margin clerk back in 1956. "Being a margin clerk meant pricing up margin accounts, seeing whether the customers had enough buying power or whether they owed us more money or stuff like that," explains Long. Before that he had been selling vitamins in Boston for Lederle Laboratories and American Cyanamid. One day, while walking to visit a customer for Lederle, Long came upon a sign that read "H. C. Wainwright & Co., Members of the New York Stock Exchange." He just walked on in and asked if they had any openings, and that was how the "The Dean" broke in.

Brenda Lee Landry makes the point that it's useful to have some background in the field you're researching. For example, she worked for Polaroid before moving into research. And Long, who always had an interest in the stock market, saved enough money while still in high school to buy shares of a small company that manufactured tabulating machines, scales, and time recorders. That fledgling concern turned out to be IBM.

As for Brenda Davis McCoy, who's been working on Wall Street for only nine years, she had no idea that she wanted to get into this line of work. But her story—one of opportunities recognized and seized—is worth listening to. Note that McCoy never thought she was too bright to start at the bottom and work her way up, or for that matter, too green to move on when the chance presented itself.

When McCoy was in college, she figured that a business administration degree would be useful in whatever field she entered. During vacations from Colby-Sawyer College, a women's school in New London, New Hampshire, McCoy worked as a temporary secretary. One of her jobs was at a small New York brokerage firm. After two weeks on the job, she was offered a permanent position when she graduated. McCoy returned to the brokerage firm as a secretary. After awhile she switched to the trading desk, and it was there that her career plans, thanks to a nasty boss, began to take shape.

As McCoy recalls it, "While I was on the trading desk, I had a problem with one of the officers who put in an order. He had asked me to buy some options on an exchange. I purchased them for him, and then he reneged. He said he never wanted them, but I knew that he had asked for them. I had repeated the order back to him right before the close. The fact that somebody could say 'That wasn't what I wanted' was enough to get me out of trading. Supposedly this sort of thing rarely happens, but it happened within a period of six months that I was on the desk. So I decided to get into research.

"I then went to Morgan Stanley. Originally I was interviewed for a job in research, but I wasn't qualified for the position. They wanted somebody with experience. I ended up in retail sales, thinking that if something opened up, I could go in and apply. Nothing opened up for a year, and I heard there was a job as a junior analyst at Mabon Nugent. I interviewed and got the job, and that's how I got started in research.

"I was working with the director of research, covering aerospace subcontractors with him. I was also doing a lot of administrative work. I was monitoring the profitability of the equity trading account daily; I was doing all the editing of the research reports that were going out of the firm, and I was overseeing the general operations of the research department.

"At Mabon they basically said, 'Okay, this is what we want you to do. Go ahead and do it. If you fail, you're out. If you stumble and trip, you're out. If you're successful, then you're all set.' "

After a successful stint at Mabon Nugent, McCoy moved on, first to Merrill Lynch and then to PaineWebber.

McCoy's hectic schedule has never allowed her time to go to graduate school for an MBA. Instead, she taught herself with books and forged ahead on her own. Now at the top of her field, an advanced degree is not a necessity. As she rightly notes, "What ultimately counts is how good you are at what you do, that is, how good you are at making people money and/or the quality of the research product."

WHAT YOU CAN MAKE

Brenda Davis McCoy started out at $20,000 when she joined Mabon Nugent in 1980. That was without an advanced business degree. MBAs, she says, can expect to come in at $35,000 to $40,000. Whatever salary you start at, you can be assured of a quick increase if you prove to have talent. At most firms, you're paid not only on the basis of what you do as a researcher, but also for any investment banking deals in which you're involved. That is, if you bring in a client who's going public or do research on a merger, you'll be compensated for that work. How high can you go? Easily into six figures, and if you're really good, as high as a million dollars annually.

Finally, though, love of the work is the big payoff. Perrin Long, Brenda Lee Landry, and Brenda Davis McCoy all exhibit greater than average energy and enthusiasm. They are, you could say, addicted to what they do. Brenda Davis McCoy perhaps speaks for all three when she exclaims, "I can't imagine doing anything else. No way!"

Robert Farrell

ANOTHER SIDE OF THE RESEARCH COIN

Robert Farrell of Merrill Lynch approaches his work as an analyst with the same enthusiasm but from a different perspective. He is one of the more rarefied breed known as market analysts. Farrell describes what he does as "the study of the forces that make stock prices move." This differs from fundamental analysis in that the technician actually studies the market itself and stocks, as opposed to the fundamentalist who studies companies, going out to see management and making judgments about an industry's fundamental and economic trends.

What Bob Farrell is looking at, then, is the behavior of the stocks themselves. In addition to using charts and computers, he brings psychology and financial history to bear on the decisions he makes. In this way, his approach differs from that of yet another type of analyst, the chartist, who tries to anticipate what will happen next solely by studying stock trends. For the market analyst, stock trends are only part of the story. Market analysis is a larger study, taking into account supply and demand and other forces and influences on the market, of psychological changes and the measure of monetary policy change, all of which impact on the market.

Bob Farrell is the very best at what he does. For an entire decade he was number one in the Market Timing category of *Institutional Investor*'s "All-America Research Team." He also was the first president of the Market Technician's Association, formed in 1972, and is well known in European and Japanese financial circles. A low-key man who tries to "play down any trappings of success" and to live "an orderly life," Farrell credits part of his renown to his position as chief market analyst at Merrill Lynch, where he's worked since 1957. He gives speeches regularly and writes a "Market Comment" that is circulated worldwide every Monday.

For Farrell, answers to the always questionable sweep of the market come from blending the technical with the psychological. "There are some very basic things about markets," he explains. "One is that they always go to extremes. . . . People create the extremes. . . . And people act more emotionally than they do rationally. . . . You are constantly trying not only to measure the extremes but to play against your own emotions in the investing process." Farrell feels that the emotional part of analysis is the most difficult to understand, and that most people make the mistake of not realizing that the market is riskiest when things look the most optimistic, and conversely, that the greatest opportunities are offered "when the majority only see the black hole."

In short, Farrell's basic philosophy is "if you can identify a clear consensus, then you know what *not* to do." As an example, he cites how things stood in 1972. Everyone, it seemed, was buying nifty fifty stocks (consumer stocks, like IBM, the drug companies, MacDonald's). These had been big bull stocks for a long time, but Farrell took the position that they should be sold. Indeed, they did go down. At about the same time, he predicted that basic industry would become a bull market. This was hardly the popular opinion of 1972, but by 1975, they did become market leaders.

When asked how you become a market analyst, Farrell admits that there aren't really any courses to teach you. Although he studied economics and finance at Manhattan College and afterwards went to Columbia University for a master's in investment finance, the people he hires come from all different backgrounds. Where you went to school and what you majored in are not of primary importance to him. What is important is some demonstrated ability to make money in the stock market, through having traded or invested your own money or showing "street smarts, that other side of the brain that you have to use in the stock market."

Farrell suggests that before going into the business you assess your strengths and weaknesses. If you are quantitative, a technical area may be perfect for you. Otherwise, you should consider another aspect of research. Most of the people Farrell hires have studied market analysis on their own. They've read books, they've practiced researching, and they've decided that just knowing what a company does is not enough for them. That's what drew Farrell to this area of research, and it's what he looks for in the people he interviews.

People, he philosophizes, have cycles, like the market. Therefore, it is not good to achieve a high level of success too quickly, since it's very hard to handle. "A stock that goes up gradually over time is the best kind of stock to own." Personal success, he says, is the same. And finally, on the philosophy of research: "See what you look at and check what you're doing." This is the motto that Robert Farrell's father taught him, and it's one he lives by now.

THE ECONOMIST

If the say-so of an analyst can affect a certain stock, then the say-so of an important economist can zing the entire stock market. The economy is certainly a subject we hear about every evening on the news. Someone's talking, that's for sure, and for the experts' opinions, it's the economists who are asked to step forward.

Traditionally, economists were academics, squirreled away in ivied halls. More recently, the field has expanded. Today economists can work independently, for places like the Claremont Economics Institute in Claremont, California, or for themselves, the way the eminent economist Alan Greenspan, now chairman of the Federal Reserve, did. Economists are found in corporations, and, of course, in government. Then there are the business economists, who work at banks and brokerage houses. Irwin Kellner is one of these.

When Irwin Kellner was eight years old he got himself a

Irwin Kellner

subscription to *U.S. News and World Report.* "I was the dullest eight-year-old kid you ever saw, but at least I knew what was going on," he recalls with a laugh. Kellner's early interests not only have remained with him but have paid off in a big way. He is now chief economist at Manufacturers Hanover Trust. And he's still reading.

"To be a good business economist, you have to have a nose for news," says Kellner. "You have to want to know what is going on minute by minute, hour by hour, day by day. I get very nervous if I can't get a daily newspaper." Kellner reads five or six newspapers a day, a dozen magazines a week, plus various reports. He's constantly looking for information, ideas, new ways of analyzing, new insights into what's going on. News to him is "not simply economic news. Anything can affect the economy, and that's why being an economist is so useful these days, because economics affects everybody, and everything affects economics. It's kind of a two-way street."

But written information isn't enough. Kellner also carries a small machine with him. It looks like a calculator with an antenna, but it's actually a service hooked up to an FM frequency.

It works twenty-four hours a day, providing all kinds of information; for example, news that as of 14:25 Greenwich Mean Time, the yen is 157 to the dollar, or that as of 10 A.M., the Dow is up 7.32.

There is no cookie-cutter job description of an economist's responsibilities. It differs too much from place to place. So let's focus on Irwin Kellner's bank and see how they do things.

First some fascinating background: Manufacturers Hanover Trust has had an economist to provide consulting services since the 1950s, when a prominent academic economist was asked to guest author the monthly newsletter. In 1958 Gabriel Hauge, who was President Eisenhower's chief economic advisor, joined Manufacturers Trust Co., the predecessor to MHT, as president. In the 1960s, once the bank's merger with the Hanover Bank was firm, Hauge developed a full time economics department, recruiting Tilford Gaines, who had been the economist at the First National Bank of Chicago. "Till" Gaines hired Irwin Kellner in 1970. In 1980, Gaines passed away, Hauge retired, and John McGillicuddy succeeded Hauge. McGillicuddy was a lawyer by training and a banker by profession. He was savvy enough to recognize that neither he nor his colleagues were economics oriented, and had the foresight to invite Kellner to join MHT's management committees so that Kellner could meet with these people. This, Kellner notes, was an important step, because it exposed him to the upper echelons of the bank on a regular basis. He points out how important it is to keep in touch, to avoid being perceived "as an ivory tower, doing the Ouija board or whatever."

Currently, MHT has about 30,000 employees located all over the world. About 2,000 or so work out of the New York City headquarters, where Kellner's office is located, and from where he reports directly to John McGillicuddy. Kellner's department consists of three dozen people, whose responsibilities include the corporate library and the domestic and international groups. Among them, these three areas "cover the waterfront" in terms of material produced for internal as well as external use.

Irwin Kellner frequently uses the word "relevant" to describe what he feels makes him and his department effective. Relevant means that he keeps in touch with his colleagues at the bank and with the public, and responds to the things he perceives to be happening around him. Although he enjoys the popularity that comes from appearing on TV and radio and having his name in print, Kellner specifies that the heart of his job is away from the public eye. "We've got many internal jobs to do," he explains. "The most important is to advise senior management as to likely trends in financial markets, in industries, where good opportunities lie, where pitfalls exist, the trend of interest rates, the stock market, developments overseas, foreign economics and foreign exchange, what the Federal Reserve is up to, what the Treasury is up to in terms of financing. We provide that kind of day-to-day guidance."

Kellner's specific responsibilities are almost overwhelming. He is on all the bank's operating committees and meets regularly with various senior people. Every other month he publishes a 100-page document explaining in great detail where things stand and forecasting where they're going, and he does the same via a bimonthly presentation to the board of directors. Twice a year, Kellner presents an analysis of seventy-five U.S. industries so that the lending officers can be advised of where good business opportunities lie. He answers "what if" questions, such as "What if the price of oil goes to $5 a barrel? How will this affect Texas?" He also writes the extremely readable monthly "Economic Report" published by MHT, as well as commentaries for the bank's weekly "Financial Digest," and serves as a contributing editor to *Bankers Monthly* magazine. As if all this weren't enough, Kellner sits on a number of outside advisory committees and is a member of his town's village planning board, thus admirably proving the old adage that the less time you have, the more you get done.

HOW AND HOW MUCH

Generally one doesn't simply step out of school a full-blown economist, though school is definitely where things begin. Economists are by far the most intellectual group on Wall Street. The noise they create comes from thinking, rather than from screaming across the trading room floor. The MBA is not as useful here as three other magic letters: Ph.D. Economics is probably the only area of Wall Street where anyone cares that you're a doctor.

A background in statistics, marketing, and market research will help. So will the ability to write and to explain things in a simple, commonsense way.

As for remuneration, "the average economist," says Irwin Kellner, "probably gets paid a lot more than the average lawyer or analyst. I suppose the hot lawyers from Harvard Law School start out at a much higher level than a fledgling economist. But if you're talking about people ten, fifteen, twenty years down the road, I would say that the average economist makes more than just about any other professional with, let's say, the exception of the investment banker." If you've been following the salaries in other chapters of this book, you'll know we're not talking chicken feed here.

HENRY KAUFMAN,
ECONOMIST

On the forty-first floor of One New York Plaza, in a beautifully furnished office with breathtaking views of New York Harbor, sat for over a quarter of a century one of the most influential economists alive today. Henry Kaufman, former managing director, member of the executive committee, and chief economist of Salo-

mon Brothers, has won a worldwide reputation for the accuracy of his predictions and the forcefulness of his views. A thoughtful man who is quite modest about his own influence, his words nevertheless can—and have—triggered major movements in the stock market. He has frequently been called upon to testify before Congress.

Born in Germany in 1927, Kaufman experienced terrifying events before his family escaped the Nazis when he was nine. He has said that "because of that experience and because of my studies, I believe that it is very important to have an orderly economic system and to have a relatively strong middle class. It is very dangerous when societies become polarized."

Before joining Salomon Brothers in 1962, Kaufman was in commercial banking and served as an economist at the Federal Reserve Bank of New York. He now runs his own consulting and money management firm.

Q: Were you always sure that you wanted to go into the financial world?

A: I was reasonably sure after my first year and a half of college that I wanted to go into the financial world. That it was specifically going to be on Wall Street, no. That only crystalized in my mind when I started to go to Columbia for my master's.

Q: What was your undergraduate degree in?

A: Economics.

Q: So you were definitely heading on that path. How does one become an economist?

A: Well, you don't become one. . . . That's one of the interesting aspects. There is no examination you take that says, 'Today you are an economist,' like you can take to become a CPA [certified public accountant].

Q: Exactly. And it's hard to become an economist at a young age.

A: Well, it depends on how you say 'at a young age.' Certainly when I went to work in a commercial bank, I was not an economist. I worked in the credit department. I was a junior lending officer. It was then I made the turn to the Federal Reserve Bank when I was just about to get my doctorate. Because of my business experience and academic training I was classified as an economist, and I worked in the research department of the Federal Reserve Bank of New York.

Q: Would you say that that is generally what defines to the outside world who might be an economist?

A: I think that the definition of an economist is a combination of academic credentials and the type of analytical work you're doing. I don't think you can be an economist having an undergraduate degree in psychology or having purely an undergraduate degree, because while you can have a major in economics, it isn't enough. You really need steps beyond that.

Q: Is there any other position on Wall Street that combines experience with this level of academic achievement?

A: You have to remember something else. What Irwin Kellner does is different from the work Henry Kaufman does. And the work that Henry Kaufman does may be different from Mr. Jones'. So when you speak of the work done by "economists," it isn't exactly the same. Sometimes the responsibilities are more or less, the area covered could be narrow or broad, so it's difficult to describe what I would call the work of the economist on Wall Street.

Q: What advice or direction would you give to young people who are moving into this world today?

A: I think there are several things I would probably say: (1) Develop good analytical skills. (2) Have a very good sense of history, which tends to be forgotten when we try to quantify everything in life. (3) Try to maintain a high degree of objectivity in the analytical work that you do. (4) Be able to make judgments not just on the basis of historical overlays, but try to recognize where there are elements of discontinuities. And finally I would say, you can get a false sense of confidence by having your views all the time coincide with the consensus view. There's very little glory you can ever get by being all the time in the consensus. The consensus usually does not spot the turning points.

CHAPTER 10

CONSULTANTS, ADVISERS, AND MANAGERS: THE SOOTHERS AND SOOTHSAYERS

M oney managers, also known as financial planners, advisers, or consultants, come in all shapes and sizes. They are organized into large firms such as Scudder, Stevens and Clark (total assets under management exceed $20 billion), and they work as one-man bands. Many banks, brokerage houses, and insurance companies offer financial planning and trust services. According to *Institutional Investor*'s August 1987 ranking of America's leading 300 institutional money managers, Prudential Insurance Co., with nearly $150 billion under management, wears the crown. The top ten list (dollar figures represent total assets in millions under management, as of December 31, 1986) gives an indication of the impressive amounts the biggest managers sift through their fingers.

1. Prudential (Newark, NJ)	$147,312
2. American Express (New York, NY)	105,290
3. Aetna Life & Casualty (Hartford, CT)	104,620
4. Metropolitan Life (New York, NY)	96,223
5. Equitable Inv. Corp. (New York, NY)	91,273
6. Merrill Lynch Asset Management (Princeton, NJ)	81,100

7. FMR Corp. (Boston, MA)	65,412
8. J. P. Morgan (New York, NY)	61,710
9. Wells Fargo & Co. (San Francisco, CA)	54,690
10. Sears, Roebuck Group (Chicago, IL)	54,609

What do money managers do? Basically, they take care of their clients' assets, investing them in the best possible way and providing extremely personalized counseling on issues ranging from tax-exempt investments to trusts and estates. You may well wonder how money managers differ from stockbrokers. In a way, the best of both are not that dissimilar in their overall approach. One obvious difference is the fee structure. Unlike a stockbroker, who takes a commission for each transaction, a money manager handles an entire portfolio for a single fee, usually half a percent to two percent of the total assets. Some managers additionally pass on the brokerage commission whenever a transaction takes place; others absorb it themselves.

Managers not affiliated with brokerage houses claim that their free agent status allows them to get clients the best deals, and that sets them apart from even the most caring broker. Finally, though, service seems to be the real distinguishing factor. Who hasn't heard an actor or a rock star refer to his personal manager and thought, "I sure wish I had someone to take care of me." Well, even if a financial planner can't be expected to pick up a client's dry cleaning, he can save the client a lot of nail biting by staying on top of his assets.

Actually, if you believe the stories, a money manager just might pick up that dry cleaning, too. Read on.

THE RICH *ARE* DIFFERENT

"The Privileged Client" reads the ad's headline, under which is a photograph of a slightly wary, extremely confident man. He wears an argyle sweater vest and his sleeves are rolled up, indicating casual self-assurance. Another ad in the same series for The Boston Company shows a slightly wary, extremely confident woman. She sits at a grand piano, her head resting against her left fist, her right hand tickling the piano keys. What exactly makes these clients privileged, you wonder? The answer: They are wealthy. If you have a few dollars in need of caretaking, The Boston Company wants to be your personal investment bankers. They'll handle investment management, personal lending, money market investments, residential mortgages, and more.

While institutional clients—foreign banks, universities, pension funds, and the like—may be an investment adviser's bread and butter, individual clients with literally more money than they know what to do with definitely sweeten the meal. In one television commercial, a cartoon man brags to a cartoon woman that he's just bought a yacht. She asks him who manages his money, and when he sheepishly replies that no one does, she is horrified. "You mean," she says, "that you're worth that much and you still don't have a personal banker?"

For those with about a million dollars to spare and an annual income of at least $250,000, a personal banker, financial planner, investment adviser, or whatever the money manager chooses to call himself is not hard to find. The polished doors are wide open. In fact, the red carpet is rolled out. Such perks as the steeply discounted holiday that Harris Trust offered its private-bank clients—the Concorde to London for a private mansion tour and then home on the maiden voyage of the refitted QE2—are not that unusual. Garden parties at museums and private showings at Sotheby's have taken place. And, believe it or not, it's been reported in none other than the *Wall Street Journal* that U.S. Trust officers have walked poodles and stored newly starched shirts in bank vaults.

What's happening here? For one thing, the days of fixed commissions are over. Now that commission rates are negotiable, many firms find it more stable and lucrative to set up a fee structure based on a single annual charge. This has caused firms who weren't before in this line of the business to start portfolio management divisions, and firms already involved in financial advising to take on clients they would have politely rejected not too many years ago. Where they once would have sneered at a mere million in assets, they now find much to do in the way of financial products and services for the "merely well-off."

So Wall Street has gone a'courtin' America's rich—of which there are more now than ever. According to Federal Reserve Board figures, the number of households with a net worth of $327,500 or more in constant 1983 dollars has shot up to 7 percent of all households from 2 percent in 1962.

This is not to say that all firms have opened their doors wide. Salomon Brothers, which never before offered accounts to individuals, has a minimum account size of $50 million. Prudential-Bache is slightly more down to earth with its $500,000 minimum. At any rate, either amount is enough to warrant better than average service.

A LOOK AT WORKING IN TRUSTS

When Interfirst and Republic, the two largest Dallas banks, merged in the second half of 1987 to become First RepublicBank Dallas, N.A., Texas became home to the largest bank in the South and Southwest. Not surprisingly, the bank's trust area, with assets of $55 billion, also ballooned into the biggest in the South and Southwest. Executive vice president Thomas D. Hogan, who is responsible for all corporate and employee benefits clients, explains the workings and opportunities of a healthy trust department:

"We basically manage people's assets, whether it's stocks and bonds, oil and gas, real estate, closely held companies, or limited partnerships, both for individuals and companies. What makes this work extremely interesting is the wide range of

Thomas Hogan

things that need managing. A company employee benefit plan needs looking after. So does a ski lodge in Colorado that is part of someone's estate.

"When you cover as broad a range of assets as we do," notes Hogan, "the opportunities for people working in the business are also broadened. What you do depends on your background and interests. But finding all the necessary ingredients in one person is very difficult. We hired a woman who had managed her family's closely held companies. She obviously understood closely held companies and the accounting and tax aspects of that. She was a real find.

"We have a staff of five who manage farms and ranches. That's all they do. Another fifty-two people manage real estate, and yet another group of eighty-four work only on oil and gas. We service 53,000 oil and gas companies. In fact, we're larger than some small oil companies. About 100 other professionals manage approximately $18 billion in securities, doing the same things that other investment firms do. We don't trade for our own account. What we do is manage other people's money."

All totaled, there are about 1,350 people statewide working

in the bank's trust function. Most of the people the bank hires these days live in Texas. This is somewhat of a change from the 1970s, when the Sunbelt was a booming area and it was easy to recruit from all over the country. What this means, though, is that opportunities abound for Texans who want to stay close to home.

You may assume that an MBA would be essential for trust work, but that isn't necessarily so. Says Hogan, "We in trust don't go after MBAs specifically. We hire individuals based on their background and experience and their ability to deal with customers. If someone has an MBA, that's fine, but if they don't, that's fine, too." A person working in the farm and ranch department will likely have either managed or grown up on a farm or ranch. On the same score, the oil and gas department has a good number of petroleum engineers and landmen who know how to drill a well. In terms of what they're looking for, "it's that straightforward," states Hogan.

Each account is overseen by an account manager, who pulls together the loose ends and makes sure that all the bases are being covered. If a single account has an oil well and a commercial property, such as a movie theater and a ranch, the account manager will coordinate with the oil and gas people and the real estate people and the farm and ranch people who work on that account.

Other types of work you can do vary quite a bit. You might start out as a junior research analyst, doing research into different companies and making recommendations on which stocks the trust people should buy for their clients. Or you could become a portfolio manager, which gives you the opportunity to actually manage money. Or you could be a trader, buying and selling stocks and bonds for clients' accounts. There also are accounting and operations positions.

Because so many of the jobs involve customer contact, there are a lot of opportunities for people who are interested in customer service. "When you're managing money for individuals," notes Hogan, "you get all kinds of questions. We may be managing money for a doctor who is too busy to manage his money, or we'll manage money for a widow or widower who has never balanced a checkbook. The latter may well call and say, 'I need to buy a new car. What kind do you recommend?' Or 'I need to buy life insurance. What kind do you recommend?' And when you're handling an estate, you get into a lot of legal issues. So we have quite a few lawyers here who work as account managers. We have a lot of ex-stockbrokers, too. We have ex-life insurance people and ex-loan officers. They didn't want to make loans anymore, but liked the customer contact aspect.

"Managing employee benefit plans is another kind of challenge. Here you're working with corporate treasurers, who are investment professionals. They're real heavyweights. It's not at all like working with the inexperienced individual who doesn't know what kind of car or life insurance to buy. The employee benefit plan might well be $1.5 billion. So it's a different level of contact that takes a different kind of expertise. It's a job for an MBA."

Trusts, then, is an area where there's room for different kinds of people from varied backgrounds. What counts is your experience and talent and interest in customer service.

BREAKING IN

You might assume—and it would make all the sense in the world—that anyone responsible for the investments of millionaires would have to be licensed. But in fact, unlike a stockbroker who is required to pass a battery of tests (see chapter 4), an individual money manager just has to hang out a shingle. This may change in the future; there's talk of it. In the meantime, it's open season.

There is a membership organization for financial planners, which lends credibility to those practicing money management.

The International Association for Financial Planning (IAFP) requires only that you agree to abide by a code of ethics and fork
over $125. It does, however, have a registry, and to be listed
there, a planner must have at least three years of planning
experience, meet educational standards, pass a written exam,
and submit references, along with a sample financial plan, to a
review committee.

Further, there's a series of exams that about 12,000 planners
have passed, which is administered by the College for Financial
Planning in Denver. Investments, estate planning, and the like
are covered. Those who pass the exams earn the title Certified
Financial Planner (CFP). Members of the IAFP are required to
enroll in the CFP course. Chartered Financial Consultant is
another title you can earn by taking an even tougher series of
tests. But again, none of these is legally necessary to practice
as a money manager. Neither is a degree in financial planning,
though some schools do offer it. All you really have to do is
convince a few millionaires that you can make money for them
with their money.

Of the 24,000 members of IAFP, the bulk (29 percent) come
from insurance backgrounds. Securities work, at 25 percent,
brings up a close second. General business runs third at 11
percent, with accounting, income taxation, banking, and real
estate each hovering in the 5 percent to 6 percent range. Corporate finance and law make up 3 percent each, and an astonishing
7 percent come from backgrounds that are not related to financial services.

Public relations counts for a lot in this end of the business.
With at least 10,000 investment advisers jockeying for more
than $1 trillion of pension and private accounts, according to
SEC data, effective advertising can be the key to success. Take
Fred Alger, described by the *Wall Street Journal* as a "go-go
money manager." Once one of Wall Street's hottest (for star
quality, he was compared to Paul Newman), Alger cooled off in
the 1970s, only to rise again in the '80s, thanks in part to a

zealous ad campaign. With the prestigious ad agency Foote Cone & Belding behind him, Alger launched in June 1986 what is believed to be, at $15 million, one of the biggest media campaigns ever undertaken by a private money manager. The impressive performance record the campaign touts is being questioned by the Securities and Exchange Commission and the New York Stock Exchange. Nevertheless, as one of the largest independent money managers, Fred Alger Management, Inc. owns a Big Board seat and claims big deal clients like PepsiCo Inc.'s pension plan and Alaska's state government.

As for the money you can make, consider that Fred Alger spent $15 million just on advertising. With $3.5 billion in client accounts, you don't have to be a math whiz to estimate his tax bracket. Even for those just starting out, remember that a 1½ percent fee on a million-dollar account comes to $15,000. Multiply that by several accounts, and the numbers add up fast. Of course, another set of numbers—how well you do with your clients' money—is what finally determines how long you'll be in business. That can be an up and down affair, as the following stories demonstrate.

RISKY BUSINESS

Mario Gabelli has been labeled a "Hit Picker" by *Manhattan, inc.* magazine. His money management firm, Gabelli Group, Inc., is a winner, having under its wing the Gamco Investors equity portfolio, which manages around $1.3 billion for 500 clients. Speaking of clients, they include John Loeb, a founder of Loeb, Rhoades & Co., and Oscar de la Renta, who needs no introduction.

Gabelli, an on-the-run, go-getter type, started out with an itch for Wall Street. As a kid he hitchhiked from the Bronx to the Sunningdale Country Club in the elite suburb of Scarsdale, New York, to caddy and pick golfers' brains about the stock market.

He bought his first stocks before hitting high school, and zoomed out of Fordham University summa cum laude with a reputation as a hustler. Moving on to Columbia for an MBA, Gabelli continued to play with stocks, magically turning practically no money into "somewhere between $11,000 and $20,000" by the time he graduated. At his first Wall Street job at Loeb, Rhoades, as a securities analyst covering the auto parts industry, he earned himself a name. It's the combination of his drive, his natural stock-picking talent, and the experience he gained as an analyst that's brought him great success.

But Mario Gabelli is, in all likelihood, savvy enough to understand that like the stock market itself, the business of managing money has its ups and downs. Forstmann-Leff Associates is a case in point. In the 1970s, it achieved one of the best performance records in the country for its institutional clients, who, by 1982, had entrusted several billion dollars to the firm. Then in 1983, the roller coaster shot down the mountain. Suddenly the stocks Forstmann-Leff had picked were all wrong; several senior portfolio managers were forced to leave, and by 1984, clients had snatched back $1.5 billion of their assets. Fortunately for this company, what went down came back up again. A composite of its accounts gained 25.2 percent in 1986, compared with the 19.8 percent advance of the Standard & Poor's 500 index. Like we've said before, the stock market is a gambler's paradise.

MANAGEMENT CONSULTING

Management consulting is not to be confused with money management. They are leagues apart. In fact, management consulting, which in the simplest terms might be defined as "someone helping you figure out how your business can be better run," probably doesn't in the strictest sense belong in this book since it's not directly related to Wall Street. Except that along with investment banking, it's the hottest area for MBAs, another of the high-paying glamour jobs young fast trackers are flocking to. (If you're hanging out in those circles, you hear management consulting being talked about all the time, so you might as well get a feel for it.)

Probably the best way is to zero in on a top management consulting firm and talk with one of its principals, specifically, one responsible for recruiting.

The firm: McKinsey & Company, Inc.

The man: Larry S. Kanarek

McKinsey & Company is one of the largest and most prestigious management consulting firms. About 1,500 professionals work out of forty-five offices throughout the world. Truly international, half the employees are not American citizens. The New York office, while not considered headquarters, holds about a quarter of McKinsey's total resources. The next biggest base is in Germany, where there are offices in Munich, Dusseldorf, Stuttgart, Frankfurt, and Hamburg. Other international offices include Amsterdam, Brussels, Caracas, Oslo, Paris, Hong Kong, Melbourne, London, Madrid, and Tokyo. In the U.S., McKinsey has offices in every major city, including Los Angeles, San Francisco, Atlanta, Chicago, Cleveland, Boston, Pittsburgh, Washington D.C., Dallas, and Houston.

McKinsey's client base is incredibly impressive—about 60 percent of the Fortune 50; 45 percent of the Fortune 100, and 35 percent of the Fortune 500 over the last three or so years. Within the business community, McKinsey is what's known as "a high value-added consulting firm," which means that the more complex the problem, the fuzzier it is, the harder it is to get your hands around, the better McKinsey is at solving it. Larry Kanarek uses this analogy to describe McKinsey: "It's a little like an automobile. Any automobile you buy can take you from here to the supermarket, we hope. At least, most can. But if you want one that just will not break down and can also take corners at 150 mph and be quiet when you do it, we like to think of ourselves in that class."

As for Larry Kanarek, he's been at McKinsey since 1980. A thoughtful, intelligent man, he works mostly in the area of service companies, some financial and some nonfinancial. What defines a service company? They are companies more service- than product-oriented, like law firms and mutual fund firms.

Q: What do you do as a management consultant?

A: That's a good question. Let me tell you what the mission of the firm is, as the firm describes it. I won't quite get this word for word, but I think you'll get the gist of it. "To work with top management of leading organizations throughout the world to improve their performance." Some of those words have been carefully chosen. "With" as opposed to "for," "top" management as opposed to "middle" management. "Organizations" so we just don't limit it to what Americans think of as corporations. The word "world" is there because it does connote that we are an international organization. And then we finally get to the bottom line, which is what our job is: to help top management improve the performance of their organization.

Q: How often are the changes you propose financial ones?

A: Rarely. A more typical example would be, "How can a major airline compete in the future in the world of deregulated airlines? What does deregulation imply to the business? What will be critical to success in the airline business on a go-forward basis? How would they position relative to some of the competition? And then finally, what should they do?" From a business standpoint [Wall Street and management consultants] do very different things. The biggest link between us and Wall Street is competition for people, not competition for clients or work.

Q: Why is management consulting so enticing to MBAs?

A: What we offer people is the opportunity to very early in their careers work on the kinds of business problems that they more typically would have to wait five, ten, or more years before they really got seriously involved with.

Q: What kinds of problems?

A: The example I just gave you is a good one. Obviously [young employees] play a role within a team here at McKinsey when they join us, and they play a junior role, but still, if you said to them, "What is on your mind today?" They would say, "What's on my mind today is how can Pan American Airlines compete in the future against Delta, American, and United." If you took the same individual and had him join Pan American Airlines out of business school, that would be a very back-of-the-mind issue. They might more typically be worried about "how should we change our frequent flyer program to attract more customers?" I think a lot of people who join us are trying to bypass the five years or more that you spend doing things like that and jump right to the big questions. So intellectual curiosity is probably paramount to what [employees] are seeking from us and also what we are looking for in them. People who just can't get a question like that out of their minds.

Q: It sounds like fun. But is it, in fact, a lot of numbers crunching and data seeking and that sort of thing?

A: It's some of that. Investment banking is what I would call heavily process-oriented in the beginning, crunching lots of numbers and then putting together lots of process-driven reports. I would guess that our people would spend dramatically less of their time doing that and dramatically more of their time thinking about that problem I just posed to you. Sure, eventually you are going to have to crunch some numbers to get a feel for what causes one airline to be profitable versus another that's not. But you're going to have to spend a lot of time thinking and learning about that business before you can even say, "What numbers would I crunch?"

The thing we don't offer is a lot of finance. So if you went through business school, and somebody said to you, "Fast, tell me what your favorite course was." And your answer was "finance," and then they said what was your second favorite course, and you answered, "Hmmm, I'm not sure." Then we are probably not the right place for you, because we just don't do only finance. If you are interested in the financial community from a broader perspective, from a marketing perspective, from a strategy perspective, from an organizational perspective, then we are fine.

Q: What would be a more intriguing answer for you?

A: If you had some trouble identifying one [course], then you're on the right road.

Q: What else are you looking for?

A: A couple of things. Although we do specialize in some industries, we sometimes don't know as much as the people themselves in that business. That means you're dealing with a chief executive officer, and you're twenty-eight years old and normally you would have gone through five or ten years [working in the corporate world] before having anything to do with that person. We're looking for someone who can sit and have a conversation with a senior manager, and indeed a middle manager, and be able to comfortably propose ideas, but also strike the right balance between putting forth our ideas and recognizing that you don't stand in the shoes of that individual who has a different perspective. Maybe the words maturity and confidence [apply]. It takes a fair dose of that to leapfrog five years of experience in the corporate world.

The other thing I would mention is a tolerance for ambiguity. When I say, "How should Pan Am compete in the deregulated airline business?" we're not able to list right now the twenty things that would be critical, the fourteen analyses we should do, and dependent upon those analyses, what the answer would be. Maybe there are a couple of people here [who could come up with the answers immediately], but by and large, not all of us could do that right away. So we need people who have the intellectual curiosity to solve that problem and a tolerance for the ambiguity that not knowing exactly the right route to get to the answer implies. . . . If you do a piece of work that takes four months, that means you spent one and one-half to two months in a state of "not defined clarity."

Q: Would a young person coming in work as part of a team?
A: Yes. It varies, but three would probably be a minimum. Four might be more typical, five or six not unusual.

Q: What salary would that new person come in at?
A: It would vary a lot with his or her background. It's hard to give you an exact answer without listing a large number of exceptions. Half the people who join us come not from business school but from industry. The salary of someone with experience would be appreciably higher than that of someone with less experience. You may also find that across consulting firms, the rate will really vary. There will be people who hire a lot of people direct from industry. There will be other consulting firms that hire only out of schools, so they have a much more standardized approach.

Q: Are the hours extremely long, as they are in so many other areas of business?
A: They are long, but I don't think they are anything like what people experience in the investment banking world. We do a survey from time to time, and what we've found is that the average person works fifty-five hours a week, plus some travel, which I think amounts to another five on average. So the range is anywhere from the high forties to the low sixties. Generally, the philosophy around here is that if you are getting into the sixties, a lot of people will start asking how can you maintain the quality of work. If you're trying to figure out what's critical to the airlines business at 11:00 at night, I can tell you that you're a lot better off going to sleep. You're more

likely to have the answer when you wake up fresh than by staying up all night thinking about it. On the other hand, fifty-five hours a week is not a short work week. If you're a hard worker by nature, it allows you to maintain other interests and a family life, and yet work hard. It's doable.

CHAPTER 11

OPERATIONS AND SYSTEMS: KEEPING THE WHEELS TURNING

The processing and support areas of Wall Street are known as operations, and it's a part of the business that couldn't be more crucial. That's because nothing would actually get done without operations. All the trades and sales and deals in the world could be made, but without operations to process them, they would float forever in never-never land. For example, after a broker makes a sale, something has to happen to keep the accounts up-to-date and post that sale. And something has to happen to settle that trade with the rest of Wall Street, because when a customer buys a financial instrument through a broker, he's buying what someone else is selling.

But operations is much more than simply processing orders. In fact, it's extremely diverse. Operations is also the overall day-to-day running of the business; it's dealing with customer needs and complaints; it's compliance, which is about keeping the proper checks and balances so that wrongdoing does not occur. One operations vice president at a major firm explains: "Operations is providing the right amount of information to the sales force and all the supporting areas so they can conduct business on a daily basis. It is providing the proper amount of controls. 'Controls' means policing yourself to make sure that the accounting is being done and the information is not accessed by the wrong individuals and that each customer is being treated properly within the rules of the industry."

Sal Campione is administrative manager of one of Merrill Lynch's branch offices at the New York Financial Center. In that capacity, he is responsible for compliance, customer complaints, and the day-to-day running of the branch. The issues he deals with include orders not being placed correctly, customers not getting their checks, stocks not being transferred. These problems come his way because his office processes orders, takes in checks, and keeps the records of the accounts. Campione explains that in most firms, operations on the branch side consists of a wire room, from which orders are commonly transmitted, cashiers, and sometimes bookkeepers. "Then in the home office," he continues, "you have many supporting areas, such as the reorganization department, which gets involved with tenders and mergers and processing of the instructions. There's a transfer department, which transfers securities, be they stocks or bonds. There's a central cashier area, which handles the processing of funds. There are so many areas, I couldn't begin to tell you all of them."

One way to divide operations positions is between those jobs that require regular contact with the public and those that are behind the scenes. People who process the orders and run the computers have historically been considered to work in the back office or back end of the business, because talking with clients is generally not part of their jobs. People who work in services deal more directly with customers, keeping them satisfied and solving their problems. Someone with a question about a statement, for example, will likely speak with an operations person in services. This is the front end of the business.

Just how important are the operations staffs? Well, in 1986, an average of more than 140 million shares of stock were traded *every day* on the New York Stock Exchange. There were more than 3,000 mergers and buyouts, worth more than $250 billion. Junk bonds alone floated in a $50 billion-plus pool. All of this activity would have been no more than a mere puff of smoke without operations people doing their jobs.

HARD WORK, LITTLE GLORY

In the hierarchy of Wall Street, operations is far from the top. Unlike investment banking, it has little cache. Unlike trading, it has few minute-by-minute thrills. Operations people are Wall Street's diligent problem solvers and engineers. They work hard, they work fast, and they are extremely skillful. They are, without question, invaluable. Yet, glory is not one of the job's rewards. Sal Campione notes that one of the struggles in operations is helping people take pride in their work.

Operations recruiters hope the image will change. "Operations is not the most attractive area," says one. "I think that's unfortunate because it's an area of challenge that many college students overlook. It's wide open, really unexplored at this point in time. As the business gets more and more sophisticated, we're developing new and more complex products and services that require convoluted processing schemes. For people who like hands-on work, there's no better way to learn the business, to see the back end of it and process it day to day. With the automation that's coming into the field, there are wonderful opportunities for people who have systems analysis backgrounds. As the compliance issues get more sophisticated, we have to make sure we have strict controls and that we're processing the business accurately and within its guidelines. We need people who will stay on top of things."

BREAKING IN

Unlike other areas of Wall Street where fairly rigid standards determine who gets hired, operations has a wide range of entry points for many different kinds of people. You may be a high school graduate who will begin your career on Wall Street as a clerk. You may be a college graduate with excellent interpersonal skills; for you, a position as a customer service representative at a branch could be perfect. An MBA might well go into operations research, working on how to restructure the flow of business to keep it as streamlined and efficient as possible.

You might come in through a formal training program, or you might apply directly for a particular position. Your skills could be analytical or computer-related or interpersonal, or a combination. The qualifications an interviewer will look for vary quite a bit, depending on whether you're planning on going into the front or back end. Overall, operations used to be a very labor-intensive business, and those working in it could count on handling a ton of paperwork. But today, thanks to computers, much of that paper pushing is done automatically, leaving people free to operate at a more sophisticated level. So where once an assembly-line type of mentality was sought, interviewers now look to attract those who can solve problems, make judgment calls, and deal on a relationship-management level.

Who is best at operations? One recruiter says, "For the services area, we're looking for people who are organized and patient. They have to be good communicators. Tact is essential, of course. Then they need to learn how the various departments work and how they fit together. For the back office jobs, again, organization is a necessity. They should be detail-oriented and accurate. People skills are less important, though we still look for people who can get along with others." Says another recruiter: "These days we often look at people with liberal arts backgrounds, rather than business backgrounds. We like their broader perspective. They tend to have more creativity and greater analytical skills than someone who has focused on just one aspect of business." And a third recruiter describes it this way: "You don't have to have been at the top of your class. What you can do counts more. For somebody who likes to get his hands dirty, doesn't mind long hours, and can live with working hard before seeing the fruits of his labors, operations is a great place to be. It's a terrific way to break in."

As for advancement, it certainly is possible in the operations area itself, and it's not out of the question to work towards breaking into another facet of Wall Street. Working from within, you might begin as a clerk, progress to a lead clerk, then a supervisor, a section manager, and eventually a manager of a department. As a sales assistant, which is considered part operations/part sales, you might well step into the sales side after a while. Some people use the connections they make in their daily work to completely jump ship; having met traders while processing their orders, for example, they go into trading.

Intern programs can help you skip a few of the more basic steps. Merrill Lynch, well known in the industry for its excellent training programs, set up an internship in operations a few years ago. Before that, most of their hiring had aimed at fulfilling specific positions. Naturally, people with skills and experience that fit those particular jobs were sought. But senior management realized that there was value in developing a pool of management talent for future positions, so they began recruiting at colleges in the New York area.

A recruiter in the initial program recalls that "the feeling was we had a lot of technical experts in operations. We had people who knew their stuff inside out, but we wanted people who could look at things in a different light, find a better way, be more flexible and not do things just because we had done them that way for the last ten or fifteen years. Plus, technicians aren't always the best people managers. We wanted to develop those who were going to be good at working with people. This program was for operations managers. These are first-line management positions or fairly senior staff positions."

That training program for operations managers offered rotational assignments in key areas to trainees. Participants learned to follow the flow of the business and were exposed to the sales side, possibly working in a branch office. One object was to help them understand the time pressures of the front office, so that once they were in the back office they'd know what was needed.

As for salaries in operations, they are traditionally lower than in other areas of Wall Street, but the range is extremely broad—anywhere from $15,000 to mid-six figures, depending on the position. A clerk will be on the low end, an MBA in a senior position can more readily count on a high-end salary.

SYSTEMS

Systems is the data processing and telecommunications arm of the business. It involves working directly with computers, providing the state-of-the-art automation and systems support that keeps operations and sales forces efficient, and the customers content. Without systems to program and maintain the computers, transactions can't be processed.

A systems programmer will make sure the computers are running smoothly and will incorporate new technology. As you might imagine, this is a highly technological position. For example, when a new product or service—and there are many all the time—is devised, someone has to come up with a way to execute it.

Getting into systems can be a very competitive venture. In addition to its internship program in operations, Merrill Lynch has a corporate systems training program that recruits both nationwide and from within the company. Of the 1,000 applicants in 1986, 42 were selected for the program. The lucky few chosen go into one of two programs. The fifteen-week systems programming class trains those with fundamental computer science knowledge to enter positions in communications programming, networking, space management, and capacity management. The twelve-week business applications class, for those with an interest but no background in programming, trains people to enter one of the business systems development departments.

Where graduates of these programs are placed depends on their preference, their performance during the program, and the openings at Merrill Lynch. Their salaries start at close to $30,000, and within three to five years, they may be making as much as $50,000.

With the competition for this program so stiff, you may well wonder what Merrill Lynch is looking for in its applicants. Not surprisingly, it's pretty much the same as you've heard throughout this book—well-rounded leaders with good analytical and communications skills. What might be surprising is that extensive knowledge of computers is not necessarily required.

There's no question that technology's influence in the world at large and most certainly on Wall Street is strengthening every day. In 1968, when the daily trading volume on the New York Stock Exchange was a mere (by today's standards) 13 million shares, the exchange had to shut down once a week, and at 2 P.M. from June to December, in order to catch up with the backlogged order flow. Now volume records are broken regularly, and the exchange doesn't miss a beat. Well-run operations and systems are the key to remaining competitive . . . and competition is Wall Street's heartthrob.

PART THREE
YOUR MOVE

CHAPTER 12

GETTING WHERE YOU WANT TO BE

N ow that you've gotten this far, you may have decided it's time to go on to business school. Or you may have determined that the best route for you is directly into a job on Wall Street. Or maybe you want to be accepted into one of the trainee or intern programs the banks offer. Wherever you are at this point, the next step is an important one, because above all, you want the door you're about to knock on to open and the opportunities to unfold before you. Unfortunately, Wall Street isn't a magic kingdom, where knowing a few secret words assures entry. No, the financial community chooses its citizens carefully. With competition both for acceptance into top business schools and for jobs stiff—very stiff—it's only the most promising players who get to join the team. *You can be one of the chosen . . . you can get what you want . . . if you proceed with knowledge— of your talents, of Wall Street's needs, and of how the two fit best.*

KNOW THY BUSINESS

"You can't name the players without a scorecard" is an old saying that couldn't be more true when it comes to the complicated world of Wall Street. Another, equally apt saying might be, "You can't play the game if you don't know the rules." Here, then, are suggestions for how you can learn who's who and what's what.

Read. Not just this book, but the books listed in chapter 13. They are not tough-to-get-through textbooks. Rather, they're genuinely engaging and lively explorations of various aspects of Wall Street life. Read the newspapers and magazines mentioned in that same chapter. Subscribe to a couple of them, if you can. It's by reading the *New York Times'* business section, the *Wall Street Journal,* and business magazines such as *Forbes, Fortune,* and *Business Week* that you'll keep up-to-date on trends and the latest-breaking news. And don't forget about the financial columns in nonbusiness publications, either. Most magazines have them. The articles that *Time* and *Newsweek* run are often particularly enlightening.

Watch TV. Now here's a tough assignment. But no kidding, there are many excellent programs that will give you the inside scoop. Networks such as CNN run business and financial programs daily. Other terrific programs, such as "Wall Street Week," are weekly. Occasionally there are special reports covering subjects of special interest. Watch for them. Also pay attention to the stock market reports that the news programs run. This is your chance not only to keep up with the news and to hear provocative discussions, but to actually see some of the people who run the Street.

Talk to People and Develop Your Network of Contacts. Never underestimate how much you can learn by talking to people. Or how much help people will be willing to give you. If you or your family has a stockbroker, get together with him or her. If your cousin, or your roommate's cousin, is a trader, give him or her a call. Talk to your economics professor (get back in touch if you've already graduated) or to the person responsible for investing your school's assets. If you're already working, meet with the person in charge of your company's pension fund. Be creative and brave in your thinking about who you know or could get to know. Don't cut off your opportunities by thinking, "Oh, she'd never want to talk to me. She's much too busy." Or, "I'd only make a fool of myself by asking dumb questions." If you've done your homework, your questions will not be dumb ones.

A young woman, who currently works as assistant to a stockbroker but who is interested in breaking into investment banking, recently had cause to take the train from New York to Philadelphia. She noticed that the gentleman sitting next to her had copies of the *New York Times* and the *Wall Street Journal* and that he was working statistical figures on a pad. He also was dressed in "banker's garb"—a dark, conservative suit, white shirt, and low-key tie. When he took a break, she politely asked if he worked in the financial industry. It turned out that he was an investment banker at a major bank. He and the woman struck up a conversation. He gave her a lot of good information, and before they parted, he invited her to call him at his office if she had additional questions. The lesson here is to seize opportunities as they present themselves. Note that the woman did not interrupt the banker while he was involved in his work, but waited for him to finish. This bit of sensitivity helped ensure the probability of a relaxed conversation.

People love to share what they know, especially if they enjoy their work. And if you make a good impression by showing enthusiasm and asking intelligent questions and listening well to the answers, chances are they will be more than happy to put you on to other people who can help you—like the head of recruitment at their firm or their old friend who heads the MBA program at Harvard.

Back to our woman on the train. She did call the investment banker, not because she really had more questions burning in her brain, but because she didn't want to lose the good connection that had been established between them. She thought up a couple of questions before dialing, was warm and friendly but got right to the point, and once again impressed the banker so much that he suggested she get in touch with the head of recruitment at his firm . . . and use his name. Now that's a contact!

Remember: The more you know, the better you'll sound at interviews. And you'll be more confident.

EDUCATION AND BACKGROUND

Despite the theory (and to some extent the reality) that you have to be a member of the Old Boy's Club to make it on Wall Street, the fact is that the place is filled with men who didn't come from the "right" families or schools or clubs, and women, who, no matter how talented, under the old rules could never have been more than secretaries. The same goes for members of minority groups who in the past could not have landed top positions. Happily, things have opened up quite a bit in recent years, and though the Street still abounds with well-educated white men, others have carved places for themselves. And things promise to get even better.

What you do need, no matter who you are and where you come from, depends a lot on what area you plan to enter. Each chapter of this book covers the specific qualities required by the jobs discussed. Investment bankers, for example, must score high in quantitative skills. Traders need to be able to make split-second decisions and work well under extraordinary pressure. Stockbrokers tend to be disciplined self-starters. However, there are some traits that move across the board, and no matter what, you'll need these to make it on Wall Street.

Since many positions on Wall Street are in large part sales jobs, it's important that you speak well, are articulate and have good grammar. You have to be able to work well with other people, too, because you will be doing just that.

As for your undergraduate major, it may not matter much at all. If you're going to crunch numbers and/or use a computer, it helps, of course, to have taken some courses, but you don't necessarily need a degree in finance or computer science. Wall Street is filled with philosophy and psychology majors. What counts most is your overall resumé. Recruiters report that they love leaders—the captain of the swim team, the editor of the newspaper, the student rep on the University Administrative Policies Committee, the choir director at church. And don't stop reading if you were only a member of the swim team, not the captain, or if you sang in your church choir, but didn't direct it. Recruiters are also looking for team players, people who have experience working with other people to make a venture successful. What they are not particularly impressed with are people (and it doesn't matter how intelligent they are) who appear to have spent their lives in solitary confinement.

Recruiters also like to see ambitious people who have held summer and holiday jobs, or better yet, started their own companies. If you delivered newspapers, that's terrific, but it's even more terrific if you introduced the route in a neighborhood that didn't have home delivery before. Anyone would be impressed to learn that for two years you sold hand-painted T-shirts made by you and a friend from your dorm room. A sales job of any kind is a real booster on a resumé that is headed for Wall Street. The work needn't have been exotic. It's fine if you worked in a record store or hawked exercise equipment over the phone or held Tupperware parties.

When it comes to personal qualities, Wall Street is one of the few arenas where aggressiveness isn't considered a negative trait. On the contrary, it's much admired. We're not talking here about biting the heads off helpless animals, but about confidence and a go-getter attitude. In the financial game, the players play to win. If you plan to make it, you'd better be competitive and tough.

But if you want to know the real secret of what makes a

recruiter sit up, it's this: enthusiasm and interest in the work. Wanting more than anything on this planet to do the job is the key to everything. Without that, it doesn't matter how good you are at everything else. No job on Wall Street is easy, and those with experience know that only people with boundless enthusiasm make the grade. The hours are long, the work often grueling. None of this seems like a sacrifice to people who love what they do. Yes, there's money to be made and to most people that's a definite incentive, but if that's the only reason you want to enter the financial world, forget it. You probably won't stick it out long enough to see the big bucks.

THE INTERVIEW

When you're going after a job, a vital part—perhaps *the most* vital part—of being chosen is the interview.

If the prospect of going on interviews seems less than delightful to you, rest assured that you are not alone. Most people feel pretty nervous about selling themselves. That is, afterall, what interviews are about—putting your best foot (and handshake and smile and spirit) forward and convincing the person sitting behind the desk that he really needs and wants you on his team.

The good news about going on interviews is that it's something you get better at with practice. The more interviews you go on and the more time you spend afterwards honestly assessing what you handled well and where you could use improvement, the stronger your style will become.

Robert Half, chairman of Robert Half International, the world's largest personnel recruiters specializing in financial, accounting, and data processing professionals, observes that "the best person for the job is the one who expresses an innate ability and willingness to do the job." Proving your ability and willingness requires knowing what you're talking about. This falls into two categories: (1) knowing what job you want and why you'd be good at it; and (2) knowing about the company, its structure and personality.

If you've read the other chapters in this book, you probably have a pretty good idea by now of what you'd like to do and think you'd be good at doing. Now grab a piece of paper and go back to the particular chapter that struck your fancy. As you reread it, write down the qualifications for the job in one column and in another column note your strengths and weaknesses as they pertain to each qualification. Remember to tie in your other work and life experiences. Here's an example: You think that being a research analyst is your cup of tea. You've learned that one part of the analyst's job is giving sales presentations, usually as part of business travel. Well, as an Army brat you moved around quite a bit, and what's more, you liked it. You're an excellent traveler who is perfectly comfortable with the notion of being in a strange city and living out of a suitcase one out of every four weeks. Plus you've won several prizes for civic oration. Talking in front of groups is old hat to you. By following this line of thinking, you've accomplished several things. For one, you've articulated two of the positive points about yourself that you will want to stress at the interview. For another, you probably have given yourself a shot of self-confidence, as in, "Gee, I really would be good at that."

As for knowing about the company in general, as well as specifically about the area for which you're applying, there are a couple of ways to get the information. First, go right to the horse's mouth; most financial institutions put out glossy, well-produced brochures and pamphlets that describe the company. They will be glad to send these to you. Ask for a history of the company, an annual report, and whatever they have about the division you want to work in. By reading this information you'll get the background you need to formulate intelligent comments and questions, and you'll get some feeling for the place. Next, if you can, talk with people who work there. Be careful not to be obvious in trying to get the inside dirt on the joint. Don't expect to get a candid answer if you ask questions like, "Is the boss really a pain in the butt?" Instead, keep your questions general and let the other person open up. Listen not only to what's being said but also to what's being implied. Finally, use all that reading and TV watching you've done to compare this firm to others.

After all this preparation, there's no chance whatsoever that you'll do something self-defeating, like ask the interviewer, "What exactly does an analyst do?"

So now that you're ready to go on the interview, how about some dos and don'ts about the big moment:

Dress Appropriately. If you were aiming for a job as an advertising copywriter, jeans and a blazer or an interesting skirt and sweater might do just fine. But the financial world is generally quite conservative, and "banker's clothes" are the norm. Men should wear a dark suit, white or light blue shirt, a non-flashy tie, and well-polished shoes. Avoid large cuff links, chains, and bracelets. If you wear an earring, consider taking it off. Women can wear a suit or a dress (no frills, please), neutral hose, and pumps with lowish heels. Keep jewelry simple; save your dangly earrings and bangle bracelets for the evening. Needless to say, everything should be clean and pressed. Your hair can be stylish, but forget about wild colors and gels that make it stick straight up. Depending on where you work, you might be able to spiff up your act somewhat after you've been on the job for awhile. But at this initial stage, opt for low key.

Be Polite. Arrive on time. Be pleasant to the receptionist, the interviewer's secretary, and anyone else you come in contact with. These people *do* count. Try to remember their names for future reference. Don't forget that secretaries have power. You have to get past them to talk to the boss. Thank the person who hands you a cup of coffee or a soda. Tell the interviewer that you are pleased to meet him. Have an extra copy of your resumé

on hand. Shake hands with the people you meet. (You've probably been taught how important a firm handshake is; well, that's
true, but a bone-crusher is overstating the point.) Make eye
contact, but not to the point of hypnotizing the interviewer.
When the interview ends, thank the interviewer, and don't daw-
dle. Keeping the conversation going once the interviewer has
ended the interview will not help you one bit.

Control the Interview. The person who controls the direction of the interview has the upper hand. This is a subtle process, and one the interviewer is well aware of. Here is definitely
where practice improves your interviewing abilities. Dorothy
Leonard of Management Recruiters, a nationwide search and
recruiting firm, recommends that you get the interviewer to
voice his or her objections and concerns so that you can turn the
interview to your favor. Robert Half suggests that you turn a
question concerning something you know little about into a
comment that highlights a strong point. It's best to keep your
answers concise. If you ramble on, you may reveal more than
you intended. Don't be afraid to answer a question with a brief
reply and then a question of your own.

Ask Questions. Be prepared to ask questions. Some you will
have thought of before the interview; others will come to you
while you are talking. Don't be shy about finding out the things
you'll need to know to figure out if this is the job for you.
However, stay away from questions like, "How soon can I
expect a raise?" Or "Do people really work eighty-hour weeks?"
Questions such as these will not convince the interviewer that
you are focused on the job itself and not just its pains and perks.

Be Realistic. Just because you've always been at the top of
your class and a varsity athlete and all that doesn't mean you're
going to be a Wall Street hotshot from the giddyup. Chances are
that even with an MBA you'll be doing some fairly drudge-like

tasks in the beginning. Don't ruin your opportunity to get a foot
in the door by thinking you already know too much to start at
the bottom. Almost everybody starts there, and it's not a bad
way to learn the ropes. And be ready to get to work right away,
if you're lucky enough to land the job, that is. People who say,
"Oh, I'd love to work for you . . . when I get back from this
two-month trip to Europe I'm taking" do not endear themselves
to busy executives who have a job to get done.

Ask for the Job. If you want it, that is. Robert Half points out
that many people make the mistake of not letting the interviewer know they are eager for the job. He recommends that
you say something like, "I'd like to work for this company and
for you. I won't let you down."

Finally, you should be aware that not all interviews are one-to-
one. There is such an animal as the group interview, in which
you are faced with a team of interviewers. Firms do this for a
variety of reasons. Some companies vote on new employees
committee-style, so they all need to meet you. Other companies
want to see how well you hold up under the gun, particularly if
you're seeking a high pressure/people-oriented position. As you
can imagine, being interviewed by a team of three or more
people can be quite a challenge.

AFTER THE INTERVIEW

Your work doesn't end the second you walk out of the room.
You've just completed phase one. What you want to do now is
assess your performance, so you'll get better and better at
interviewing. How did you hold up? Which questions threw you?
Where could you have come off stronger? Also think about what
you learned about the firm. Is this a place you'd like to work?
Is the position that's being offered right for you?

Whatever you think about how well or how poorly you did, about whether you loved the company or never want to grace its corridors again, write a note to the person you met with— brief and not too formal. Try not to make it sound like a form letter. It helps if you refer to something that was said or that happened during the interview. Avoid being cute or overly clever.

If you want the job, call after a few days have passed. Robert Half suggests that you come up with some excuse to talk, such as "Oh, by the way, at the interview we discussed blah blah and I want to say that . . ." Never, Half says, ask for the job during this call.

If the job is offered to you, think hard about whether it's the right move for you. Will you learn a lot? Is there room for advancement? Look at whom you will be working with. You may not love the work you'll be doing, but it could be worth it if you'll be working for someone you admire. A good boss can become a mentor, and a mentor is a precious friend to have. Consider whether this job is a good steppingstone for you. Will it help you move on? Finally, though looking for a job is hard work, and a foot in the door is better than standing cold on the street, say no if the job isn't right for you. You'll find something else.

SUMMER JOBS, INTERNSHIPS, AND TRAINING PROGRAMS

Working in a financial institution is a great way to get experience, to beef up your resumé, and for that matter, to find out whether a career on Wall Street is what you want in reality. If you attend a school that has work-study or winter term programs, try to set up at least one round of work in a financial institution. If you're wondering how to spend your summer vacation, think about working on Wall Street.

There are a couple of ways to find out how to plug into a

temporary job. First, contact your placement office and/or adviser. Find out what programs are available and whether financial institutions recruit on your campus. Next, talk to everyone you know and anyone you don't know but can get to. (See the contacts section of this chapter for how to go about it.) Third, write directly to the banks and firms. Tell them what you're looking for, and ask what they have available and how to apply.

Temporary, holiday jobs are not to be confused with another kind of temporary job: the analyst programs in investment banking. These are the two-year positions offered generally to men and women who have just graduated from college, described in detail in chapter 3. Despite the term "analyst," the people in analyst programs are not learning how to be research analysts (described in chapter 9). They are learning how to be investment bankers, and they are being paid handsomely for this training—as much as $50,000 a year. Every bank operates its analyst program a little differently. You can get an idea, though, of what an analyst program is like by looking at First Boston's program.

You should know right off that First Boston is one of the top Wall Street firms. Its headquarters are on Park Avenue in New York (not, as you might assume, in Boston), and its reach is international. It is, in short, one of the most sought after banks, and going after a position there is a highly competitive procedure. Remember this daunting statistic: In 1986, 400 of the 1,250 graduates-to-be of Yale applied to First Boston for jobs in investment banking. Obviously there's something really attractive about this bank, which chooses, from all its applicants, about 100 for the program.

First Boston has a helpful pamphlet that describes its analyst program. As the pamphlet explains, "Analysts in corporate finance begin their careers at First Boston with an eight-week training program that teaches the fundamentals of accounting and finance, and a two-week orientation to the firm and investment banking. Public finance analysts start with a three-week orientation program and attend biweekly training seminars throughout their first year."

There are a number of ways you can structure your experience at First Boston. If you're in the corporate finance area you may opt to specialize in what's called a functional area. That's mergers and acquisitions, mortgage finance, project finance, corporate restructurings, high-yield finance, and leasing and asset finance. Or you may specialize by industry, working in the areas of technology, energy, financial institutions, health care, media, retailing, or utilities. Other specialties include international finance and product development. If you just can't decide on one area to develop your expertise, you may choose to work as a generalist. Public finance analysts, on the other hand, have four choices; they can work in the areas of health care and higher education, housing and student loans, public power, or infrastructure finance.

What is First Boston looking for in the people it accepts into its analyst program? Four qualifications are stressed:

Excellent analytical and writing skills
Strong academic records
Initiative, commitment, and creativity, as demonstrated through work or extracurricular activities
Ability to work effectively with others in an intense and demanding environment

Not surprisingly, the nine men and women featured in the pamphlet are graduates of top schools—Harvard, Dartmouth, University of Pennsylvania, Amherst, Yale, Princeton, and Stanford. Firms like First Boston actively recruit at schools such as these. What's more surprising are their majors, which range from economics to political science to English. So once again, the point is made that your major matters less than your overall achievements and abilities.

If you don't attend one of the schools where firms like First

Boston recruit, don't assume you're out of the race. You're not. You just have to get out there with your resumé and contact the firms yourself. It can be done, and it is done all the time.

The analyst programs are not the only training programs offered to talented college grads. Use the same tactics described earlier in this chapter to find out what opportunities are available in your chosen area.

BUSINESS SCHOOL

You'd have to have been asleep at the wheel not to have realized by now that an MBA goes with the Wall Street territory. Most positions absolutely require this degree; and even in those rare cases where it's not required, an MBA will still put you in a better position, not only to get the job, but also to negotiate the best salary.

Although you certainly can, there's no reason why you have to leapfrog from undergraduate to graduate school. In fact, most people don't; the average age of business students is mid-twenties, with lower and upper ages ranging from twenty to fifty. Business schools actually prefer candidates who have a couple of working years under their belts. Of course, they also consider other factors, such as your academic record, your GMAT (Graduate Management Admissions Test) scores, your application (including the essays), your recommendations, and your interview.

How do you pick which school you want to attend? Patricia Lang, associate dean of admissions at the Graduate School of Business, Columbia University, points out that people who have already been employed are often influenced by their colleagues. Career advisers and professors (either current or former) also exert an influence, as does the media—articles in magazines, for example.

One good way to begin researching graduate business schools

is to contact the Graduate Management Admissions Council (11601 Wilshire Blvd., Los Angeles, CA 90025-1746, (213) 478-1433). In addition to sponsoring the GMATs and publishing a guide to MBA programs, this organization holds national MBA forums, where you can gather information that will help you make your decision.

There are quite a few different things you'll want to consider when choosing a business school. Here are some of them:

Reputation. With 70,000 or so new MBAs marching into the marketplace each year, where you get your degree is just as important as having the degree at all. *Business Week* (March 24, 1986) reported this chilling statistic: "Fewer than a third of the more than 650 schools in the U.S. offering the MBA degree meet even the minimum standards of accreditation set by the American Assembly of Collegiate Schools of Business (AACSB)."

Placement Statistics. What is the school's record in helping students find good jobs after graduation? Do firms recruit on campus? What have the starting salaries of graduates been?

Teaching methods. What methods does the school subscribe to? Are they basically theoretical? Or do they lean heavily on case histories? Are they compatible with your style of learning?

Curriculum. Is the curriculum flexible or strict? Does it make sense to you?

Professors and Staff. Who teaches at the school? Are there any heavyweights?

Location. Where's the school located? Is it the best place for you to spend the next two years? Do you like the campus? How's the overall environment?

Cost. Almost always a factor. Can you afford the school? Will they give you aid if you need it?

In the battle of the best business schools, Harvard has long reigned. Indeed, when Louis Harris & Associates polled 488 senior executives in February 1986, a whopping 43 percent named Harvard as the best business school in the nation. But the B-school Superbowl gets played every academic year, and these days other schools, such as Stanford, are winning big points.

In its cover story on business schools, *Business Week* (March 24, 1986) listed twenty leading B-schools, along with some extremely useful figures. Here are the schools and the most interesting of that information:

SCHOOL	APPLICATIONS ACCEPTED (%)	1985 GRADS (FULL-TIME)	COMPANIES RECRUITING
California (Berkeley)	27	249	160
Carnegie-Mellon	39	124	140
Chicago	30	504	234
Columbia	29	590	300
Cornell (Johnson)	48	235	150
Dartmouth (Amos Tuck)	23	141	150
Duke (Fuqua)	67	212	135
Harvard	18	780	342
Indiana	34	332	300
MIT (Sloan)	29	193	141
Michigan	53	350	330
New York University	44	362	200
Northwestern (Kellogg)	23	603	300
Pennsylvania (Wharton)	29	710	400
Rochester	53	251	85
Stanford	9	309	238
Texas (Austin)	41	343	330
UCLA	24	370	200
Virginia (Darden)	43	206	208
Yale	20	150	140

Tuitions at these schools average around $11,000 a year, except in the cases of state schools, such as the University of California at Berkeley, the University of Indiana, and UCLA, where they're more in the $5,000 a year range. School budgets (which are good to look at because they give some indication of how much money each school has to pay its professors and provide facilities and tools for its students) vary from a modest $4 million (Dartmouth's Amos Tuck, which nevertheless has an excellent reputation) to an impressive $100 million (Harvard, of course).

A FINAL WORD BEFORE YOU START

Sure, Wall Street is a fast, hard game. Sure, it's phenomenally competitive. But don't forget that there are many different ways to get into the game. And don't forget that every team can always use another terrific player. The opportunities are out there, and they always will be, for those who truly want to be on the field rather than in the stands. If you're one of those people—go for it. The champagne celebration will follow.

CHAPTER 13

RESOURCES

Exchanges

The various exchanges located throughout the U.S. are centers of trading action. Knowing where they are will help give you an idea of how the action is spread across the country. A number of the exchanges have pamphlets and brochures they'll be glad to send you for the asking. It's recommended that you take advantage of this. By far the largest registered securities exchange is the New York Stock Exchange. In addition to the information the NYSE can send you, they offer a fascinating free tour in which you actually get to see how the floor operates. Contact them directly for the tour schedule.

Here is a listing of the exchanges:

REGISTERED SECURITIES EXCHANGES

American Stock Exchange, Inc.
86 Trinity Place
New York, NY 10006
(212) 306-1000

Boston Stock Exchange
One Boston Place
Boston, MA 02108
(617) 723-9500

Chicago Board Options Exchange (CBOE)
LaSalle at Van Buren
Chicago, IL 60605
(312) 786-5600

Cincinnati Stock Exchange.
205 Dixie Terminal Bldg.
Cincinnati, Ohio 45202
(513) 621-1410

Intermountain Stock Exchange
373 South Main St.
Salt Lake City, Utah 84111
(801) 363-2531

Midwest Stock Exchange
120 South LaSalle St.
Chicago, IL 60603
(312) 368-2222

New York Stock Exchange, Inc.
11 Wall St.
New York, NY 10005
(212) 656-3000

Pacific Stock Exchange, Inc.
301 Pine St.
San Francisco, CA 94104
(415) 393-4000
      and
618 South Spring St.
Los Angeles, CA 90014
(213) 614-8500

Philadelphia Stock Exchange, Inc.
1900 Market St.
Philadelphia, PA 19103
(215) 496-5000

Spokane Stock Exchange
243 Peyton Bldg.
Spokane, WA 99201
(509) 624-6132/800-541-5558

FUTURES EXCHANGES

Amex Commodities Corp.
86 Trinity Place
New York, NY 10006
(212) 306-1424

Chicago Board of Trade
141 West Jackson Blvd.
Chicago, IL 60604
(312) 435-3500

Chicago Mercantile Exchange
30 South Wacker Dr.
Chicago, IL 60606
(312) 930-1000

Chicago Rice & Cotton Exchange
444 West Jackson Blvd.
Chicago, IL 60606
(312) 341-3078

Coffee, Sugar & Cocoa Exchange, Inc.
4 World Trade Center
New York, NY 10048
(212) 938-2800

Commodity Exchange Inc.
4 World Trade Center
New York, NY 10048
(212) 938-2900

Kansas City Board of Trade
4800 Main St.
Kansas City, MO 64112
(816) 753-7500

MidAmerica Commodity Exchange
444 West Jackson Blvd.
Chicago, IL 60606
(312) 341-3000

Minneapolis Grain Exchange
102 Grain Exchange Bldg.
Minneapolis, MN 55415
(612) 338-6212

New York Cotton Exchange
4 World Trade Center
New York, NY 10048
(212) 938-2650

New York Futures Exchange
20 Broad St.
New York, NY 10005
(212) 656-4949

New York Mercantile Exchange
4 World Trade Center
New York, NY 10048
(212) 938-2222

Philadelphia Board of Trade
1900 Market St.
Philadelphia, PA 19103
(215) 496-5555

NEWSPAPERS AND MAGAZINES

Unless you're really hooked on Wall Street and eat financial
news like candy, it's not absolutely necessary to read each of
these publications all the time. It is a good idea, though, to keep
up with them. You never know when a piece will appear on the
very firm you've got your sights set on. And it would be a
terrible gaff to have someone at an interview refer to the latest
insider trading scandal only to have you scratch your head and
say, "Gee, I hadn't heard about that." On the other hand, it
never hurts to be able to say, "That was a terrific article on your
firm that the *Journal* ran last week."

BARRON'S NATIONAL BUSINESS & FINANCIAL WEEKLY
Financial Weekly
World Financial Center
200 Liberty St.
New York, New York 10048
(212) 416-2000

BUSINESS WEEK
McGraw-Hill Publishing Co., Inc.
1221 Avenue of the Americas
New York, New York 10020
(212) 997-1221

FORBES
Forbes, Inc.
60 Fifth Ave.
New York, New York 10011
(212) 620-2200

FORTUNE
Time Inc.
1271 Avenue of the Americas
New York, New York 10020
(212) 586-1212

INSTITUTIONAL INVESTOR
Institutional Investor Inc.
488 Madison Ave.
New York, New York 10022
(212) 303-3300

NEWSWEEK
Newsweek, Inc.
444 Madison Ave.
New York, New York 10022
(212) 350-2000

TIME
Time Inc.
1271 Avenue of the Americas
Rockefeller Center
New York, New York 10020
(212) 586-1212

NEW YORK TIMES
The New York Times Co.
229 W. 43rd St.
New York, New York 10036
(212) 556-1234

WALL STREET JOURNAL
Dow Jones
420 Lexington Ave.
New York, New York 10170
(212) 808-6960

U.S. NEWS & WORLD REPORT
U.S. News & World Report
2400 North St. NW
Washington, DC 20037
(202) 955-2000

MOODY'S, STANDARD & POOR'S, AND VALUE LINE
   Serious stock pickers and industry followers turn to these
three key references for a detailed view of companies and investments. They are quite technical, but once you get the hang
of them, they are also extremely useful.

BOOKS

There are numerous books on all aspects on Wall Street, many
of them excellent, some of them dumb at best and dishonest at
worst. This list does not attempt to cover the waterfront; instead, it points out books that may, for one reason or another,
be particularly useful to you at this time. Lots of books are
directed toward the investor, and though none of those is included on this list, you may want to peek at a few—for two
reasons: (1) they will present the "buy-side" point of view; and
(2) if you don't yet have a working knowledge of financial instruments and the wide variety of investment options, now's the
time to learn. As you look through books on your own, it's a
good idea to check their copyright dates; the Wall Street scene
is changing so fast that only books written recently are likely to
give current information.

Aliber, Robert Z. *The International Money Game.* (New York: Basic
   Books, 1983)
   A good introduction to the international money system, including
discussions of floating currency and international money markets.
Remember, though, that this book was written pre-Big Bang, Lon-
don's 1986 deregulation.

Allison, Eric W. *The Raiders of Wall Street.* (New York: Stein & Day, 1986)
Explores the reasons why corporate raiders such as T. Boone Pickens and Saul Steinberg have been so successful. How they started and moved up, their trades and deals, how they choose their targets, and the controversy surrounding their work.

Appleton, Dr. William S. *It Takes More Than Excellence: A Harvard Psychiatrist's Guide to Success in Business.* (New York: Prentice Hall, 1986)
Enumerates the qualifications needed on Wall Street; also reflects upon problems, issues, and rewards of working with others in an office environment.

Asman, David, and Adam Meyerson. *The Wall Street Journal on Management.* (New York: Plume, 1985)
Aimed at the entrepreneur, this covers not only Wall Street, but other areas of business as well. Future venture capitalists will be particularly interested, as will independent types who plan to strike out on their own.

Auletta, Ken. *Greed and Glory on Wall Street: The Fall of the House of Lehman.* (New York: Warner, 1986)
The fascinating and well-written story of how, through the machinations of a few individuals, the venerable Lehman Brothers lost its independent status and was folded into Shearson American Express.

Bloch, Ernest. *Inside Investment Banking.* (New York: Dow Jones & Irwin, 1986)
Nuts and bolts: investment banking, underwriting, mergers and acquisitions, venture capitalists, and various strategies that go with an understanding of the market.

Bord, Ray, and Fran Moody. *Breaking in: The Guide to Over 500 Top Corporate Training Programs.* (New York: Stonesong Press, 1985).

A guide to 500 corporations (not all of them financial firms) that offer training programs. Included in each listing is a description of the company and information about its training program and preferred qualifications for applicants.

Doerflinger, Thomas M., and Jack L. Rivkin. *Risk and Reward: Venture Capital and the Making of America's Great Industries.* (New York: Random House, 1987)
An exploration of how investors, entrepreneurs, and venture capitalists together created some of America's great industries— railroads, steel, telephones, automobiles, and computers—and contributed to the growth of corporate America. How new ventures are financed and how backers can make or break a fledgling firm.

Downes, John, and Jordan Elliot Goodman. *Dictionary of Finance and Investment Terms.* (New York: Barron's, 1985)
Over 2,500 finance and investment terms defined and explained. An invaluable, must-have reference.

Eaton, Bruce. *No Experience Necessary: Make $100,000 a Year as a Stockbroker.* (New York: Simon & Schuster, 1987)
Written by the former senior training consultant for Merrill Lynch, this is a straightforward assessment of brokerage. Chapters include: "A Day in the Life of a Broker," "Learning the Business," and "Do You Know What It Takes."

Fay, Stephen. *Beyond Greed.* (New York: Viking, 1982)
The larger-than-life, true story of the silver failure that took place between the Hunts of Texas and the House of Saud.

Hisrich, Bob, and Eugene Bronstein. *The MBA Career: Money on the Fast Track to Success.* (New York: Barron's, 1983)
For the after-MBA stage, this guide explores programs, gives job descriptions and names of firms, and provides helpful hints for landing a job.

Johnston, Moira. *Takeover: The New Wall Street Warriors.* (New York: Arbor House, 1986)
The story of the new breed of Wall Street warriors who are on the front lines of the multibillion-dollar struggles for control of major corporations. This is the world of mergers and acquisitions, and its players: investment bankers, arbitrageurs, lawyers, proxy fighters, institutional investors, PR people, and the raiders themselves (Carl Icahn, T. Boone Pickens, Jr., and Sir James Goldsmith).

Kleinfield, Sonny. *The Traders.* (New York: Henry Holt & Co., 1983)
An account of the human and professional sides of trading at the various exchanges.

Little, Jeffrey B., and Lucien Rhodes. *Understanding Wall Street.* (New York: Liberty House, 1980)
A good introduction to Wall Street; information is provided on types of investments, basic terminology, and the history of Wall Street. Does not concentrate on what's needed to break in.

McCormick, Mark H. *What They Don't Teach You at Harvard Business School: Notes from a Street-Smart Executive.* (New York: Bantam, 1984)
Effectively applied, this book provides an interesting perspective on the subtle aspects of business not learned in B-school. Discusses such aspects as taking advantage of timing, paying attention to the competition, and "reading" people.

Pickens, T. Boone, Jr. *Boone.* (New York: Houghton Mifflin, 1987)
The master corporate raider, head of the Mesa Limited Partnership, tells his own story, how a shy boy from a small Oklahoma town spun a $2,500 investment into the nation's largest independent petroleum company, and a huge personal fortune. Also discusses his takeover attempts of oil giants Cities Service, Gulf, Phillips, and Unocal.

Simpson, Anthony. *Money Lenders: Bankers and a World of Turmoil.* (New York: Viking, 1981)
Pre-Big Bang, this book nevertheless provides helpful information about Eurodollars, the global marketplace, and aspects of international banking.

Slater, Robert. *The Titans of Takeover.* (New York: Prentice Hall, 1987)
The behind-the-scenes story of corporate raiders, arbitrageurs, and mergers and acquisitions people, including Carl Icahn and T. Boone Pickens.

Sobel, Robert. *Inside Wall Street.* (New York: W. W. Norton, 1982)
An excellent source for a general overview of Wall Street. History, aspects of researching financial instruments, information on the New York Stock Exchange are provided.

Spooner, John D. *Sex and Money.* (New York: Dell, 1985)
A cynical but lively and often valid look at the world of the stockbroker.

Stewart, Marjabelle Young, and Marion Fox. *Executive Etiquette: How to Make Your Way to the Top with Grace and Style.* (New York: St. Martin's, 1979)
A guide to getting along in the workplace while moving up the ladder. Emphasis is placed on the importance of quality performance, teamed with appearance and behavior and the development of personal skills.

Stumpf, Stephen A. *Choosing a Career in Business.* (New York: Simon & Schuster, 1984)
A guide to entry-level positions in the financial world. Gives strategies for various types of career moves.

Tamarkin, Bob. *The New Gatsbys: Fortunes and Misfortunes of Commodity Traders.* (New York: Quill, 1985)

A vivid, tough portrayal of the world of the commodity trader. Includes such chapters as: "Us Against Them," "A Psychic Battlefield," "Why Isn't $1 Million Enough?" and "Pit Brats."

Zweig, Philip L. *Belly Up: The Collapse of the Penn Square Bank.* (New York: Crown, 1985. Ballantine, 1986.)

Written by a Wall Street Journal reporter, this is the grim, true story of the fall of Penn Square.

INDEX

A B O U T   T H E   A U T H O R

Cheri Fein is a journalist, fiction writer and poet whose work has appeared in publications as diverse as *Connoisseur* and *Glamour, Ms.* and *Mademoiselle, Partisan Review* and *Ploughshares.* She is the recipient of many awards, including a creative writing fellowship from the National Endowment for the Arts. In addition to the book reviews she has written for the *New York Times Book Review,* the *Washington Post Book World,* and the *Village Voice,* Ms. Fein is the author of three nonfiction books.